T0328876

THOMAS GRAY

ODE ON THE SPRING

AND

ELEGY IN A COUNTRY CHURCHYARD

EDITED BY

D. C. TOVEY, M.A.

Cambridge :
at the University Press
1921

CAMBRIDGE
UNIVERSITY PRESS

University Printing House, Cambridge CB2 8BS, United Kingdom

Cambridge University Press is part of the University of Cambridge.

It furthers the University's mission by disseminating knowledge in the pursuit of education, learning and research at the highest international levels of excellence.

www.cambridge.org
Information on this title: www.cambridge.org/9781107594753

© Cambridge University Press 1921

First edition 1901
Reprinted 1916, 1921
Re-issued 2015

A catalogue record for this publication is available from the British Library

ISBN 978-1-107-59475-3 Paperback

CONTENTS

This Edition of these two Poems is taken from Gray's *English Poems* edited by D. C. Tovey and published in the Pitt Press Series.

INTRODUCTION.

THOMAS GRAY was born on the 26th of December, 1716. His father was Philip Gray, said to have been a scrivener or broker. This man amid other sources of income owned a house and shop in Cornhill which in the year 1706, or thereabouts, was let to two sisters Mary and Dorothy Antrobus. At this date, approximately, Philip was on the eve of marriage with Dorothy, and their marriage-contract left her still a partner with her sister in the business (millinery), they paying Philip Gray rent for his shop, and the three, apparently, living together in the house connected with it. Dorothy Gray was financially independent of her husband, with whom she lived unhappily, and from whom in 1735 she endeavoured to get a separation. She had at this time given birth to twelve children, of whom Thomas, the fifth, was the only survivor; the rest had died in infancy; and the future poet might have shared their fate but that his mother opened one of his veins with her own hand.

To his mother Gray owed his education both at Eton and Cambridge. There is nothing to contradict the impression made by Mrs Gray's 'Case for Counsel' (1735)[1] that his father was a brute, and perhaps crazy[2]. The straitened circumstances

---

[1] First published by Mitford. Gray's *Works*, vol. I. pp. xcvi sq.

[2] 'He daily threatens he will pursue her with all the vengeance possible, and will *ruin himself to undo her, and his only son*; in order to which he hath given warning to her sister to quit his shop, where they have carried on their trade so successfully, which will almost be their ruin' &c. Mrs Gray's 'Case for Counsel.'

of the poet's earlier years, compared with the ease and comfort with which he lived at Cambridge after his father's death, point to the inference that it was not poverty but callous selfishness that made Philip Gray put the task of providing for his son upon this 'careful, tender mother.'

Dorothy Gray's brother, William Antrobus, was an assistant master at Eton, and thither in 1727 Gray was sent, perhaps[1] as his pupil. There is some reason to believe that Mrs Gray was a humble friend of Lady Walpole[2] (the daughter of Alderman Shorter); this perhaps was the starting point of the friendship at Eton between Horace Walpole and Gray. Two other names are linked with this friendship, Richard West and Thomas Ashton. West was the son of the Lord Chancellor of Ireland, and, on his mother's side, the grandson of Bishop Burnet. At Eton he was reckoned the most brilliant of the little *coterie*, there known by the name of the Quadruple Alliance. His early death in 1742 was to Gray a never-forgotten sorrow[3]. Ashton, the least interesting member of this group, entered into holy orders, and achieved some promotion in the Church; but became at last estranged from Walpole, his affection, as Walpole suggests, cooling when his friend ceased to be a prime minister's son, and hopes of preferment in that quarter lapsed in consequence.

Both Gray and Walpole were delicate children; and it speaks well for the Eton of that day that they were allowed to follow their own studious bent unmolested, and that our poet loved those fields in which he moved with little or no share or skill in the sports of boyhood.

Gray left Eton for Cambridge in 1734. He became a pensioner at Peterhouse. Another uncle, Robert Antrobus, had been a fellow of that college[4]. Gray had little sympathy with

---

[1] See note 4 *infra*.

[2] See *Gray and His Friends*, pp. 4, 5, 60, 61.

[3] *Gray and His Friends*, pp. 15—17.

[4] Dr Bradshaw says that this *Robert* was Gray's tutor at Eton. Mason also affirms that Gray's tutor there was a fellow of S. Peter's

Cambridge studies, as then pursued; he gave up attending lectures; and in 1739 he went with Horace Walpole for a continental tour, of which Walpole bore the principal expense. That incompatibility of temper which travel so often discovers broke out in an acute form at last, and ended in the separation of the friends at Reggio in 1741[1]. Gray went off with two friends of his and Walpole's, John Chute and Francis Whithed, to Venice, and thence returned home, accompanied only by a servant, arriving in London on the 1st of Sept. 1741. His father died on the 6th of November following.

Gray spent some time between London and Stoke Pogis (whither his mother and his aunt Mary Antrobus had gone to live with their widowed sister, Mrs Rogers), and finally, after hesitating between his old college and Trinity Hall[2], returned to Peterhouse (this time, I believe, as a fellow-commoner), in the autumn of 1742, graduating as LL.B. in 1744. His choice, even before he started on his foreign travels, was ostensibly the bar, but he never made any attempt to pursue that vocation, preferring that life of secluded study to which the possession of a competency enabled him to devote himself.

In November 1745 a reconciliation was effected between Gray and Walpole[3]. The young men had never lost esteem for each other. Walpole especially wrote of Gray kindly even during their estrangement, and mentioned him always with

College (*William* was of King's). Since Robert died in 1729, it is clear that Gray, even if he entered Eton under him, must have passed into other hands before he left school. Perhaps from Robert to William?

[1] A close examination of Gray's correspondence would show that Ashton was a mischief-maker in this matter, probably by retailing to Walpole some unkind comments received from Gray.

[2] I have not space to exhibit the evidence on which these statements are based. Gray's correspondence has never been published with any care for chronological sequence; if it ever should be, it will be found that my statements are correct.

[3] A lady is said to have done much to bring this about. This lady I conjecture, doubtfully, to have been a maiden sister of John Chute.

pride and affection, modified only by gentle complaints of his censorious temper.

From this point the history of Gray is more and more identical with that growth of his mind and of his studies which I have tried to trace in my notes. In 1756 he removed from Peterhouse to Pembroke College on the other side of the street, in consequence of a cruel practical joke played upon him by some fellow-commoners, of which the college authorities refused to take sufficient notice. It should be remembered that he was at this time the famous author of the *Elegy*.

In 1762 he attempted indirectly through Walpole and Sir Henry Erskine, a creature of Lord Bute's, to obtain the Professorship of Modern History at Cambridge. It was given to a Mr Brockett, of Trinity, who had been tutor to Sir James Lowther, son-in-law of the prime minister. In 1766 it was offered to Gray unsolicited, probably at the suggestion of Stonhewer, secretary to the Duke of Grafton. Gray accepted it, but delivered no lectures.

Cambridge was in the main the poet's residence during the whole of his life from 1742 to his death in 1771. The year 1759 was spent by him for the most part in London, in researches in the British Museum; he stayed at times with his mother and aunts at Stoke Pogis; and was occasionally the guest of Walpole, Wharton and other friends. He visited different parts of England and Scotland, and was one of the first Englishmen to appreciate the beauty of lake and mountain scenery. He died in Pembroke College on the 30th of July, 1771, and was buried in Stoke Pogis Churchyard, in the same tomb with his mother.

In the notes attention has designedly been called to the hostile criticisms of Johnson upon Gray's poetry. I have felt that this prejudice is not to be dismissed in a word; like all Johnson's antipathies it is well worth investigating. I have referred it elsewhere to the dislike which the man who has written for his bread is inclined to feel towards the man who writes for his own amusement, and there was certainly in the matter of literary taste and bias a line of demarcation which might be overstepped, but which is very clearly traceable, between the adventurers who came up to town to live by their wits, and the *dilettantists* who from a secure social or academic position could make or welcome experiments. The hardworking man of letters believed in the conditions under which he had slowly made his way to fame. It is only his prose style that can be said to be quite distinctive of Johnson, by virtue perhaps of an inevitable law which in one direction or the other makes the style the man. When he wrote 'London' and 'The Vanity of Human Wishes,' the language of the age was, a few conventionalisms apart, rapidly becoming the language of its poetry, the very thing which Gray declared it never could be for a permanence, except in French. A less exact observer than Gray, Johnson had not perhaps noticed how largely not only Dryden but Pope had borrowed from the older diction of Shakespeare and Milton[1]. At any rate he set his face against any attempt to repeat that example; he hated these borrowings from antiquity, these things strange yet not new, whether they were offered him by Gray or by Percy, whether they appeared with 'strutting dignity,' as he would call it, in a revived ornateness, or in the simplicity of ballad poetry; and he struck out both to the right and to the left. Accustomed as we are to think of the simple pathos of the *Elegy* as clothed in language sufficiently trite, it should startle us to find that the man whose name is often used as a synonyme for pompous diction found it blemished by that defect, as well as by offensive archaisms and affected inversions. We get to the root of Johnson's objections in one clear instance which sets his meaning beyond mistake. He made two versions of a chorus of the Medea. One of these is an attempt without bias; it represents his own notion of how the thing ought to be done; he gave it to Burney for his History of Music :—

> The rites deriv'd from ancient days
> With thoughtless reverence we praise,

---

[1] See Gray to West, April, Thursday, 1742 (quoted in part on *Agrippina*).

The rites that taught us to combine
The joys of music and of wine,
And bad the feast and song and bowl
O'erfill the saturated soul;
But ne'er the Flute or Lyre apply'd
To cheer despair or soften pride,
Nor call'd them to the gloomy cells
Where Want repines and Vengeance swells,
Where Hate sits musing to betray
And Murder meditates his prey.
To dens of guilt and shades of care
Ye sons of Melody repair,
Nor deign the festive dome to cloy
With superfluities of joy.
Ah, little needs the Minstrel's power
To speed the light convivial hour;
The board with varied plenty crown'd
May spare the luxuries of sound.

Here there is scarcely a word that would seem affected in the conversation either of Johnson's day or our own; and the same may be said of most of Johnson's verse no less than of Goldsmith's. But now take the same passage rendered by him in the style, as he conceived it, of the Elegy:

Err shall they not, who resolute explore
Times gloomy backward with judicious eyes;
And scanning right the practices of yore,
Shall deem our *hoar progenitors* unwise.

They to the dome where smoke with curling play
Announced the dinner to the regions round,
Summon'd the *singer blythe* and *harper gay*
And aided time with *dulcet-streaming* sound.

The better use of notes, or sweet or shrill,
By quiv'ring string, or modulated wind,
Trumpet or lyre—to their *harsh* bosoms *chill*
Admission ne'er had sought, or could not find.

Oh ! send them to the *sullen* mansions *dun*
His baleful eyes where Sorrow rolls around ;
Where *gloom-enamour'd* Mischief loves to dwell
And Murder, all *blood-bolter'd*, schemes the wound.

Where *cates luxuriant* pile the spacious dish,
And purple nectar glads the festive hour,
The guest without a want, without a wish,
Can yield no room to Music's soothing pow'r.

Mrs Piozzi calls this a burlesque and a parody, and that it
was written, as she says, 'with some merry malice' is undoubtedly true; an absurd touch here and there, as in the
second line, betrays this; otherwise we might almost take it
quite seriously, indeed an unguarded critic might be betrayed
into quoting it as distinctively Johnsonian. But the adjectives
following their substantives, the archaisms, the epithets double
and hyphenated and always indispensable, belong to Gray, not
to Johnson, and have much to do with that charge of obscurity
which sounds so strange to modern ears. The inversions too
of subject or object with the verb are Gray's, and no one else
perhaps in his day would have written, as he undoubtedly did,

Awaits alike th' inevitable hour,

to the bewilderment of printers ever since. But chiefly by
reviving and consequently enlarging our poetic vocabulary
does Gray appear as an innovator. He was of all the in-
novators of his day in this respect perhaps the most conscious
and deliberate, a fact which justifies the pains which Mitford
and others have taken in tracing his diction to its probable
sources.

In another and later direction the results of Gray's effort, so
tardy and in volume so scanty, were still more noteworthy. The
fact that the 'Progress of Poesy' and the 'Bard' were published
together has obscured for us the generic difference between
them. Before he wrote the 'Bard' Gray's mind had received a
new bias; he had begun those studies in Scandinavian literature
which modified his treatment of that poem. His characteristic

hesitation over it might have left it a belated fragment but for the music of Parry, the blind Welsh harper, which gave him a stimulus just in time. Its effect, especially in combination with the two 'Norse Odes,' was far-reaching indeed. In the huge Ossianic mirror Gray saw, without recognizing, his own distorted image. Yet he had helped to prepare a public for Macpherson. The wand which the student-poet waved so cautiously, in bolder hands conjured up wider visions, many of which were only phantasmagoric. But when the world had shaken off these portentous shadows, it found its poetic horizon mysteriously enlarged; it was in this case a happiness that there is no controlling power to keep due measure between a novel experiment in literature and its possible effect. Between Gray and Scott intervene not only the Ossianic Mist, but the *Reliques* and that tide of Romanticism of which Percy and Macpherson, involuntary associates, opened the floodgates; a tide which returned to us in greater volume from abroad. Still the two poets somehow contrive to join hands; in that spiritual succession which criticism loves to trace back, we pass by such names as Mason and Warton and find in the 'Bard' and the 'Norse Odes' the first memorable exemplars of new studies put to poetic use by a mind delicate, fastidious, and a little hampered by conventions belonging to a very different tradition; and with these and 'Christabel' we link the 'Lay of the Last Minstrel.' It was given to Gray and to Coleridge, minds most critical, most receptive, but in the way of production most inert, to stimulate and fashion the labours of a spirit more robust, and capable, in that new world of romance in which Gray was a pioneer, of working with surprising rapidity and a versatile energy almost inexhaustible.

I. ODE ON THE SPRING.

Lo! where the rosy-bosom'd Hours,
　　Fair VENUS' train appear,
Disclose the long-expecting flowers,
　　And wake the purple year!
The Attic warbler pours her throat,
Responsive to the cuckow's note,
　　The untaught harmony of spring:
While whisp'ring pleasure as they fly,
Cool Zephyrs thro' the clear blue sky
　　Their gather'd fragrance fling.　　　　10

Where'er the oak's thick branches stretch
　　A broader browner shade;
Where'er the rude and moss-grown beech
　　O'er-canopies the glade,
Beside some water's rushy brink
With me the Muse shall sit, and think
　　(At ease reclin'd in rustic state)
How vain the ardour of the Crowd,
How low, how little are the Proud,
　　How indigent the Great!　　　　20

Still is the toiling hand of Care:
   The panting herds repose:
Yet hark, how thro' the peopled air
   The busy murmur glows!
The insect youth are on the wing,
Eager to taste the honied spring,
   And float amid the liquid noon:
Some lightly o'er the current skim,
Some shew their gayly-gilded trim
   Quick-glancing to the sun.   30

To Contemplation's sober eye
   Such is the race of Man:
And they that creep, and they that fly,
   Shall end where they began.
Alike the Busy and the Gay
But flutter thro' life's little day,
   In fortune's varying colours drest:
Brush'd by the hand of rough Mischance,
Or chill'd by age, their airy dance
   They leave, in dust to rest.   40

Methinks I hear in accents low
   The sportive kind reply:
Poor moralist! and what art thou?
   A solitary fly!
Thy Joys no glittering female meets,
No hive hast thou of hoarded sweets,
   No painted plumage to display:
On hasty wings thy youth is flown;
Thy sun is set, thy spring is gone—
   We frolick, while 'tis May.   50

IX. ELEGY WRITTEN IN A COUNTRY CHURCH-YARD.

THE Curfew tolls the knell of parting day,
    The lowing herd wind slowly o'er the lea,
The plowman homeward plods his weary way,
    And leaves the world to darkness and to me.

Now fades the glimmering landscape on the sight,
    And all the air a solemn stillness holds,
Save where the beetle wheels his droning flight.
    And drowsy tinklings lull the distant folds:

Save that from yonder ivy-mantled tow'r
    The mopeing owl does to the moon complain   10
Of such as, wand'ring near her secret bow r,
    Molest her ancient solitary reign.

Beneath those rugged elms, that yew-tree's shade,
    Where heaves the turf in many a mould'ring heap,
Each in his narrow cell for ever laid,
    The rude Forefathers of the hamlet sleep.

The breezy call of incense-breathing Morn,
    The swallow twitt'ring from the straw-built shed,
The cock's shrill clarion, or the echoing horn,
    No more shall rouse them from their lowly bed.   20

For them no more the blazing hearth shall burn,
    Or busy housewife ply her evening care :
No children run to lisp their sire's return,
    Or climb his knee the envied kiss to share.

Oft did the harvest to their sickle yield,
    Their furrow oft the stubborn glebe has broke :
How jocund did they drive their team afield !
    How bow'd the woods beneath their sturdy stroke !

Let not Ambition mock their useful toil,
    Their homely joys, and destiny obscure ;   30
Nor Grandeur hear with a disdainful smile
    The short and simple annals of the poor.

The boast of heraldry, the pomp of pow'r,
    And all that beauty, all that wealth e'er gave,
Awaits alike th' inevitable hour.
    The paths of glory lead but to the grave.

Nor you, ye Proud, impute to These the fault,
    If Mem'ry o'er their Tomb no Trophies raise,
Where through the long-drawn isle and fretted vault
    The pealing anthem swells the note of praise.   40

Can storied urn or animated bust
    Back to its mansion call the fleeting breath ?
Can Honour's voice provoke the silent dust,
    Or Flatt'ry soothe the dull cold ear of death ?

Perhaps in this neglected spot is laid
  Some heart once pregnant with celestial fire;
Hands, that the rod of empire might have sway'd,
  Or wak'd to extasy the living lyre.

But Knowledge to their eyes her ample page
  Rich with the spoils of time did ne'er unroll;　　50
Chill Penury repress'd their noble rage,
  And froze the genial current of the soul.

Full many a gem of purest ray serene,
  The dark unfathom'd caves of ocean bear:
Full many a flower is born to blush unseen,
  And waste its sweetness on the desert air.

Some village-Hampden, that with dauntless breast
  The little Tyrant of his fields withstood,
Some mute inglorious Milton here may rest,
  Some Cromwell guiltless of his country's blood.　　60

Th' applause of list'ning senates to command,
  The threats of pain and ruin to despise,
To scatter plenty o'er a smiling land,
  And read their hist'ry in a nation's eyes,

Their lot forbad: nor circumscrib'd alone
  Their growing virtues, but their crimes confin'd;
Forbad to wade through slaughter to a throne,
  And shut the gates of mercy on mankind,

The struggling pangs of conscious truth to hide,
  To quench the blushes of ingenuous shame,　　70
Or heap the shrine of Luxury and Pride
  With incense kindled at the Muse's flame.

Far from the madding crowd's ignoble strife,
  Their sober wishes never learn'd to stray;
Along the cool sequester'd vale of life
  They kept the noiseless tenor of their way.

Yet ev'n these bones from insult to protect
  Some frail memorial still erected nigh,
With uncouth rhimes and shapeless sculpture deck'd,
  Implores the passing tribute of a sigh.   80

Their name, their years, spelt by th' unletter'd muse,
  The place of fame and elegy supply:
And many a holy text around she strews,
  That teach the rustic moralist to die.

For who to dumb Forgetfulness a prey,
  This pleasing anxious being e'er resign'd,
Left the warm precincts of the chearful day,
  Nor cast one longing ling'ring look behind?

On some fond breast the parting soul relies,
  Some pious drops the closing eye requires;   90
E'en from the tomb the voice of Nature cries,
  E'en in our Ashes live their wonted Fires.

For thee, who mindful of th' unhonour'd Dead,
  Dost in these lines their artless tale relate;
If chance, by lonely contemplation led,
  Some kindred spirit shall inquire thy fate,—

Haply some hoary-headed Swain may say,
  "Oft have we seen him at the peep of dawn
Brushing with hasty steps the dews away
  To meet the sun upon the upland lawn.   100

[Him have we seen the Green-wood Side along,
   While o'er the Heath we hied, our Labours done,
Oft as the Woodlark piped her farewell Song,
   With whistful eyes pursue the setting Sun.]

"There at the foot of yonder nodding beech,
   That wreathes its old fantastic roots so high,
His listless length at noontide would he stretch,
   And pore upon the brook that babbles by.

"Hard by yon wood, now smiling as in scorn,
   Mutt'ring his wayward fancies he would rove,   110
Now drooping, woeful-wan, like one forlorn,
   Or craz'd with care, or cross'd in hopeless love.

"One morn I miss'd him on the custom'd hill,
   Along the heath, and near his fav'rite tree;
Another came; nor yet beside the rill,
   Nor up the lawn, nor at the wood was he:

"The next, with dirges due in sad array
   Slow thro' the church-way path we saw him born.—
Approach and read (for thou can'st read) the lay,
   Grav'd on the stone beneath yon aged thorn."   120

[There scatter'd oft, the earliest of the Year,
   By Hands unseen are Showers of Violets found;
The Redbreast loves to build and warble there,
   And little Footsteps lightly print the Ground.]

THE EPITAPH.

Here rests his head upon the lap of Earth
   A Youth, to Fortune and to Fame unknown.
Fair Science frown'd not on his humble birth,
   And Melancholy mark'd him for her own.

Large was his bounty, and his soul sincere,
   Heav'n did a recompence as largely send: 130
He gave to Mis'ry all he had, a tear,
   He gain'd from Heav'n ('twas all he wish'd) a friend.

No farther seek his merits to disclose,
   Or draw his frailties from their dread abode,
(There they alike in trembling hope repose,)
   The bosom of his Father and his God.

NOTES.

I. ODE ON THE SPRING.

THIS poem is touchingly connected with the story of Gray's friendship with Richard West. In his Commonplace Books (sometimes called the Stonehewer MSS.) preserved at Pembroke College, Cambridge, Gray's transcript of it bearing the title "Noon-tide, an ode" has the note "at Stoke, the beginning of June 1742 sent to Fav: not knowing he was then Dead." It was a response to the verses which West, whom, playing on his name, Gray was wont to call 'Favonius' (the Western Wind), had sent him (May 5, 1742), invoking 'May.' These verses Gray acknowledged on the 8th of May; received another from West in cheering strain enclosing translations from Catullus on the 11th; responded brightly on the 27th; and must have written once more about a week later a letter enclosing the poem before us, which was returned to him unopened[1], West, as he afterwards discovered, having died on the first of June. The first of Gray's and the last of West's original efforts in English Verse were on the same theme, and both these kindred spirits as they wrote thought more of friendship than of fame.

Gray's MS. at Pembroke does not, as far as I remember, exhibit any essential variation from the text of Mason, except perhaps in the more frequent use of capitals: accordingly the text is here given from vol. I of Mason's 4 vol. edition 1778, as printed by A. Ward and sold by Dodsley and others.

Mitford has illustrated the poem with his customary care and diligence, and almost all the fire of quotation which has been brought to bear on it has been derived from his magazines. In 1768 Gray

---

[1] See *Gray and His Friends*, pp. 164—172.

added notes of his own, which must be taken to indicate the passages which he really had in mind ; and to these are added the more precise references which Mitford supplied.

Mason inferred from the title 'Noon-tide' that Gray originally intended to write three poems descriptive of Morning, Noon, and Evening. He remarks that the *Elegy* opens with a picture of Evening, and the fragment on *Vicissitude* with a picture of Morning. We have seen however under what conditions the *Ode on the Spring* was in fact produced ; and it is perhaps not possible to say at what date Gray transcribed the poem and headed it otherwise. But if, as I think, his transcript contains the reading of ll. 19, 20 as we here print it, the correspondence which Mason attributes to original design was an afterthought, if it entered into Gray's mind at all[1]. It is not the time of day which is Gray's subject in any of the three poems ; but it would be very like him designedly to distinguish them by adapting in each case the hour to the theme.

It may be, as Mitford affirms, that the Ode is founded on 'Horace's Ode *ad Sestium* (I. iv.)' ; but the resemblance goes no further than this, that Horace passes from a description of the return of Spring, not much resembling Gray's, to reflections on the brevity of human life.

    I. **the rosy-bosom'd Hours.** The expression is traced by Wakefield to Milton, *Comus* 986 :

> "Along the crispèd shades and bowers
> Revels the spruce and jocund Spring :
> The Graces and the rosy-bosomed Hours
> Thither all their bounties bring."

Thomson, as Mitford indicates, had already borrowed from Milton in

> "The *rosy-bosomed Spring*
> To weeping fancy pines."   (*Spring*, 1010.)

Did Milton take the word from the Greek ῥοδόκολπος, which is to be found in a Lyric fragment preserved by Stobaeus (*Ecl.* I. 174) as an epithet of εὐνομία? It may be difficult to fix the sense of ῥοδόκολπος as used in this fragment ; but whether Milton had come across it or not, he probably used 'rosy-bosomed' after the analogy of ῥοδοδάκτυλος 'rosy-fingered' as an epithet of Morn in Homer. So also Thomson and Gray ; Dr Bradshaw's suggestion that the meaning may be 'with bosom full of roses' after the analogy of 'rosy-crowned,' *Progress of Poesy* 28, is

---

[1] For, with the earlier reading of these lines, the poem was certainly called "*Ode on the Spring.*" See n. ad loc.

not so likely, though it is a little sanctioned by Mitford's quotation from Apuleius, "Horae *rosis* et caeteris floribus *purpurabant* omnia."

2. **Venus'.** Of course a dissyllable. Cf.

> "The fickle pensioners of Morpheus' train."

> Milton, *Il Penseroso* 10.

train. Mitford quotes *Hymn to Venus* II. 5, and *to Apollo*, l. 194, for the Hours as attendants on Venus. His citation from Hesiod, *Works and Days* l. 75, is not apposite; there the Hours are described as decking *Pandora*.

3. **long-expecting.** Dryden, *Astraea Redux* 122:

> "Frosts that constrain the ground, and birth deny
> To flowers that in its womb *expecting* lie."

> Rogers.

4. **the purple year.** Classical as this phrase seems, the nearest approach to it is "ver purpureum" in the tenth book of Columella, which he composed in hexameters after the manner of the *Georgics*. Whether any English poet before Pope in his *Pastorals* (1709) said 'purple year' I cannot discover; he probably did most to make the phrase familiar. Milton, *Lycidas* 141, writes "purple all the ground with vernal flowers"; and the word in this connection is used generally of all bright colours. Cf. n. 1 ad fin.

5. **The Attic warbler.** Cf. out of many classical instances Propertius II. 16. 5, 6

> "Non tam nocturna *volucris* funesta querela
>   *Attica* Cecropiis obstrepit in foliis."

But the passages more or less in Gray's mind and fixing his phraseology are Milton, *Paradise Regained* IV. 245

> "See there the olive-grove of Academe,
>   Plato's retirement, where the *Attic bird*
>   *Trills her thick-warbled* notes the summer long"

and Pope, *Essay on Man* III. 33

> "Is it for thee the linnet *pours his throat*?"

Mark Pattison here, after noting Gray's imitation, adds "Pope more correctly *his throat*, the female bird having no song. Milton errs in the same way, *Par. Lost* 4. 600

> 'All but the wakeful nightingale:
>   She all night long her amorous descant sung.'"

But surely the 'error' is inevitable, at any rate in connection with the nightingale: the poets are still under the spell of the old-world legend of the daughter of Pandion king in Attica,—Philomela (or her sister

Procne as some said) transformed into a nightingale, and lamenting for
ever her sorrows. Even Keats who quite ignores the legend, and like
Gray seems to find more joy than sadness in the bird's song, betrays this
'error' in gender when he writes, "thou, light-wingèd *Dryad* of the
trees." Byron is on the safe side, because he follows the *Persian* fable:

> "For there the Rose, o'er crag or vale,
>
> Sultana of the Nightingale,
>
> The maid for whom his melody,
>
> His thousand songs are heard on high,
>
> Blooms blushing to her lover's tale."

> *The Giaour.*

In Matthew Arnold the old Greek story and the consequent offence
against natural history return together full-fledged:

> "Dost thou again peruse
>
> With hot cheeks and sear'd eyes
>
> The too clear web, and thy dumb sister's shame?
>
> Dost thou once more assay
>
> Thy flight, and feel come over thee,
>
> Poor fugitive, the feathery change
>
> Once more, and once more seem to make resound
>
> With love and hate, triumph and agony,
>
> Lone Daulis, and the high Cephissian vale?"

Pattison l.c. adds "To 'pour' song or sound is an expression used by
many poets after Simonides of Ceos, *Fr.* 153. 8 ἡδὺ πνεῦμα χέων." He
suggests also that the harshness of the metaphor 'pour *his throat*' is
subdued by the repetition of the idea in the next line

> "Loves of his own and raptures *swell the note.*"

But it still remains a bold and questionable trespass upon such expressions as "liquidum tenui gutture cantat avis" (Ovid, *Amores* I. 13. 8)
from which it is derived. Gray would not have employed it if Pope had
not given it vogue.

6, 7. **note...spring.** Thomson (strangely misquoted in this place
by Luke) writes (*Spring* 579):

> "...while I deduce,
>
> From the first note the hollow cuckoo sings,
>
> The symphony of Spring."

'Harmony' is in apposition with the general sense of ll. 5, 6, a
construction corresponding to a common use of the Greek accusative; it
is scarcely exact to say, with Dr Bradshaw, that it is in apposition with

throat and note. Gray may have had Ovid, *Tristia* III. 12. **7**, 8 somewhere in his mind :

> " Prataque pubescunt variorum flore colorum
>   *Indocilique* loquax gutture *vernat* avis."

14. **O'er-canopies.**

> "A bank......
> O'er-canopied with luscious woodbine.**"**

    Shakespeare, *Mids. Night's Dream* [II. i. **251**].
Gray (who here follows the text of Pope).

 17. **reclin'd,** says Dr Bradshaw, "agrees with *me*, l. 16." Surely not ; if the Muse can be imagined to sit with the poet, she can also be imagined to recline in rustic *state.* Gray gives her the honours proper to the scene ; and treats her as he might some woodland goddess or fairy queen.

 18. **ardour.** Horace's *civium ardor*, *C.* III. iii. **2.**

 19, 20. " 'How low, how indigent the Proud,
>   How little are the Great.'

Thus it stood in Dodsley's *Miscellany* [**1748**], where it was first published. The author corrected it on account of the point of *little* and *great.* It certainly had too much the appearance of a Concetto, though it expressed his meaning better than the present reading." Mason.

 23. Cf. Pope, *Essay on Man* I. **210**—"the green myriads in the *peopled grass.*"

 26. **the honied spring. Let us hear** Johnson on this passage, by way of warning against hasty criticism :

"There has *of late* arisen a practice of giving to adjectives, derived from substantives, the termination of participles ; such as the *cultured* plain, the *daisied* bank ; but I was sorry to see, in the lines of a scholar like Gray, the *honied* Spring."

 To this Lord Grenville (*Nugae Metricae*, privately printed) quoted by Mitford in his *Life of Gray* has replied : " A scholar like Johnson ought to have remembered that *mellitus* is used by Catullus, Cicero and Horace, and that *honied* itself is found both in Shakespeare and Milton." [*Henry V.* I. i. 50, "to steal his sweet and honeyed sentences." *Samson Agonistes* 1066, "the bait of honied words." Nearer still to Gray "quaint enamell'd eyes That on the green turf suck the *honied* showers," *Lycidas* 140, and "the bee with *honied* thigh," *Il Penseroso* l. 143.] Lord Grenville further remarks that "the ready conversion of our substantives into verbs, participles, and participial adjectives is of the very essence of our tongue." He cites *inter alia* such words as *plough, witness, ornament*

(we may add *father*) ; and notes how participles of verbs thus derived
pass into adjectives as in *winged, feathered, thatched*; and how there is
the closest analogy between these participial adjectives, and words like
honied, daisied, tapestried, slipper'd, which differ from the others only in
not being referable to any yet established verb. He instances *sugared*,
as an epithet the use of which was probably anterior to that of the verb,
of which it appears to be the participle. He points out that Johnson's
canon would banish from the language such expressions as *four-footed,
open-hearted, short-sighted, good-natured*; the '*well-envyned frankelein*'
of Chaucer; and *even-handed, high-flighted, trumpet-tongued, full-voiced,
flowery-knitted, fiery-wheel'd* of Shakespeare or Milton.

27. **And float…noon.** "Nare per aestatem liquidam," Virgil. *Georg.*
lib. IV. [59]. Gray.

30.   "……sporting with quick glance
     Shew to the sun their wav'd-coats dropt with gold."
              Milton's *Par. Lost*, b. VII. [410]. Gray.
Milton here speaks of *fishes*, in describing the six days of Creation.

31. **To Contemplation's** &c. "While insects from the threshold
preach &c." M. Green in the *Grotto.* Dodsley's *Misc.* vol. V. p. 161.
Gray.

Matthew Green died in 1737. He printed and gave away a few
copies of the *Grotto* in 1732. It was "written under the name of Peter
Drake, a fisherman of Brentford." The subject of the poem was otherwise called the Queen's Hermitage, or Merlin's Cave at Richmond, a fancy
or folly of Queen Caroline's ; of it Stephen Duck (hence 'Peter Drake')
the thresher-poet was Librarian; the cave and its custos were both the
objects of Pope's ridicule. See *Gray and His Friends*, p. 89 n. In a
letter to Walpole of 1748 Gray says that the thought on which his *Ode
on Spring* turns is "manifestly stolen" from the *Grotto*; "not," he adds,
"that I knew it at the time, but having seen this many years before, to
be sure it imprinted itself on my memory, and, forgetting the Author, I
took it for my own." (Cf. note on Ode III. l. 21.)

It is noteworthy that one of Gray's favourite French poets, his contemporary Gresset, had the same characteristic as Green, a sort of careless
facility and diffuseness often akin to prose ; and that Gray, in borrowing
from both, compresses their thoughts, whilst he adopts a more stately
and artificial manner :

     "While insects from the threshold preach,
        And minds disposed to musing teach;
        Proud of strong limbs and painted hues,

> They perish by the slightest bruise;
> Or maladies begun within
> Destroy more slow life's frail machine:
> From maggot-youth, thro' change of state,
> They feel like as the turns of fate:
> Some born to creep have liv'd to fly,
> And chang'd earth's cells for dwellings high:
> And some that did their six wings keep,
> Before they died, been forced to creep.
> They politics, like ours, profess:
> The greater play upon the less.
> Some strain on foot huge loads to bring,
> Some toil incessant on the wing:
> Nor from their vigorous schemes desist
> Till death; and then they are never mist.
> Some frolic, toil, marry, increase,
> Are sick and well, have war and peace;
> And broke with age in half a day,
> Yield to successors, and away."

But this is only one of the many motives in Green's poem, which in discursiveness and variety is in the manner of the 17th century, Andrew Marvell's manner for instance, whereas Gray has *but* this leading notion, to which the whole poem is focuss'd.

Wakefield, says Mitford, has traced Gray's stanza to Thomson's *Summer* 342 sq. I give the passage as it stood in 1730:

> "Upward and downward, thwarting and convolved,
> The quivering nations sport; with tempest wing,
> Till Winter sweeps them from the face of day.
> Even so luxurious men, unheeding, pass
> An idle summer life in fortune's shine—
> A season's glitter! [In soft-circling Robes
> Which the hard hand of industry has wrought
> The human insects glow; by Hunger fed,
> And chear'd by toiling Thirst,] they rowl about
> From Toy to Trifle, Vanity to Vice
> Till, blown away by death, oblivion comes
> Behind, and strikes them from the book of life."

The thought in brackets was omitted in 1744 and 1746, and the whole passage as we now read it strikingly resembles Gray's stanza. Gray praised Thomson grudgingly; and, if he was indebted to him, would never have acknowledged as much to Walpole, who sneered at Thomson habitually. Both Green and Gray before they wrote their own lines had in all probability read the passage in *Summer* in the form in which it is cited above.

42. **The sportive kind reply.** We must defer to the overwhelming weight of authority which takes 'kind' as a substantive and 'reply' as a verb here. The 'sportive kind' are therefore the insect youth on the wing, sporting with quick glance, the 'quivering *nations*' as Thomson calls them, whose murmur seems to the poet to shape itself in words. It is certainly better to suppose this to be the primary meaning than to say with Dr Bradshaw "sportive kind, men of the world, and gay friends of Gray's, whom he supposes to mockingly reply to his moralizing." Nevertheless this view is sanctioned by the author of the version in *Arundines Cami*, who writes :

"Forte (?) *aliquis* cui cura joci, cui ludere cordi est" &c. where the Latinity and the interpretation are both questionable.

II. THE ELEGY.

In August **1746** Gray writes to Wharton from Stoke, "The Muse, I doubt, is gone, and has left me in far worse company; if she returns, you will hear of her." And from the same place to the same correspondent, on the following Sept. **11** (after the account of Aristotle quoted by Matthew Arnold in his Essay on Gray) : "This and *a few autumnal Verses* are my Entertainments dureing the Fall of the Leaf." I know of no poem but the *Elegy* to which these fitful efforts of the 'Muse' are likely to belong.

Once more from Stoke, on June **12, 1750**, Gray writes to Walpole, "I have been here a few days (where I shall continue a good part of the summer) and having put an end to a thing, whose beginning you have seen long ago, I immediately send it to you. You will I hope look upon it in the light of a thing with an end to it ; a merit which most of my writings have wanted, and are likely to want."

That this 'thing' was the *Elegy* there can be no doubt. Walpole could not have seen the 'beginning' of it at an earlier date than Nov. 1745,—the date, as I have shown (*Gray and His Friends*, p. 7), of his reconciliation with Gray,—except we adopt the extremely bold hypothesis that the *Elegy* was begun before the quarrel, that is to say before, as far as can be ascertained, Gray had written a line of original English verse.

Mason, in his *Memoirs of Gray*, speaking of the date August 1742, that month of exceptional efflorescence in Gray, says, " I am inclined to believe that the *Elegy in a Country Churchyard* was begun, if not concluded, at this time also. Though I am aware that, as it stands at present, the conclusion is of a later date; how that was originally, I have shown in my notes on the poem." (The four stanzas which, according to Mason, originally ended the poem will be found *infra*, n. on l. 72.)

Of the MS. of the *Elegy* in which these four stanzas occur, called by Dr Bradshaw the 'Original,' by Mr Gosse the 'Mason,' and by Mr Rolfe the 'Fraser' MS. 100 copies were printed in 1884. The MS. does *not* end with these four stanzas, but contains them *with* the conclusion as we now read the poem[1]. Gray added his after-thoughts without effacing the lines for which he meant to substitute them: this is characteristic of him, for he had a great aversion to erasure. That he could not have intended the *second* and *fourth* of these stanzas to remain is clear, because they are remodelled in ll. 73—76, and ll. 93—96; but the four stanzas, however beautiful, are abrupt, considered as the last lines of the poem. When Gray sent the poem to Walpole in 1750, he could congratulate himself that the 'thing' had really an *end* to it, both as compared with its previous state and with the fragmentary *Agrippina*.

Walpole did not at first accept the account of the date of the poem, submitted to him by Mason before the Memoirs of Gray went to press. He writes, Dec. 1, 1773:

" The 'Churchyard' was, I am persuaded, posterior to West's death [1742] at least three or four years. At least I am sure that I had the twelve or more first lines from himself above three years after that period, and it was long before he finished it."

And yet Mason appears to have satisfied Walpole that the opinion expressed in the Memoirs was correct, for Walpole writes to him Dec. 14, 1773, that his account of the *Elegy* puts an end to his criticism on the subject.

---

[1] Mason says, 'In the first manuscript copy of this exquisite poem I find the conclusion different from that which he afterwards composed.' He has only inferred that the four stanzas were the original *conclusion* and endeavours thus to force this inference upon his readers.

Walpole was surely *complaisant*, if Mason induced him, against his better memory, to admit that the *Elegy* could have been concluded, in any sense, in 1742. What evidence could Mason have adduced that it was even begun in that year? Not certainly the testimony of Gray himself, for if Mason could have relied upon that he would have let us know it. He must, I think, have persuaded Walpole that the three or four opening stanzas were not, as Walpole supposed, written shortly before he saw them, but, like the fragment of *Agrippina*, had long been laid aside. But would not Gray have told Walpole this, and would not Walpole, whose own impressions receive much confirmation from Gray's hints to Wharton in 1746, have recollected it?

If, as seems probable, Gray gave Walpole these opening stanzas not by letter, but when the reconciled friends were together, whether in '45 or in the summer of '46, when he was at Stoke and 'seeing Walpole a great deal' (to Wharton Aug. [13] 1746), Walpole would have no *documentary* evidence to oppose to Mason's representations whatever they may have been, and might easily have been induced by a man more conceited and obstinate than himself to mistrust his memory of what had happened twenty-seven years before. And that Mason's notions of the date of the *Elegy* were in no way modified by what Walpole told him, leads one to mistrust those notions altogether. However this may be, there can be no doubt that a goodly part of the *Elegy* was composed at intervals between August 13, 1746, and June 12, 1750. That the death of Gray's maiden aunt, Mrs Mary Antrobus, at Stoke, on Nov. 5, 1749, stimulated Gray to resume the poem may be true, and is more probable than that the death of his uncle Rogers in October 1742 prompted him to begin it.

Lastly, Gray's heading to the Pembroke MS. is 'Elegy written in a Country Churchyard 1750.' He has given in the same MS. minute details as to the editions of the *Elegy*; if he had written a substantial part of it as early as 1742 (a year so memorable to him), he might have been expected to record this.

Of the *Elegy* there are three copies in Gray's handwriting extant; the one mentioned already, which may be considered as the rough draft; this was purchased in 1875 by Sir Wm. Fraser. It will be referred to in these notes, after Mr Rolfe, as the Fraser MS. Another copy was in Wharton's possession, and accordingly is in the Egerton MSS. in the British Museum. I have never seen it, for when I consulted the Wharton Letters there, the *Elegy* had been taken out for exhibition. Of the third, the MS. at Pembroke College, Cambridge, I made such memoranda as a brief opportunity admitted. Many therefore of the Various Readings here recorded are given on the faith of previous editors.

Walpole was so delighted with the *Elegy* that he showed it about in manuscript with the result that it got into the hands of the enterprising publisher. Accordingly Gray wrote to Walpole from Cambridge, Feb. 11, 1751 :

"As you have brought me into a little sort of distress, you must assist me, I believe, to get out of it as well as I can. Yesterday I had the misfortune of receiving a letter from certain gentlemen (as their bookseller expresses it) who have taken the Magazine of Magazines into their hands. They tell me that an *ingenious* Poem called Reflections in a Country Churchyard has been communicated to them, which they are printing forthwith; that they are informed that the *excellent* author of it is I by name, and that they beg not only his *indulgence*, but the *honour* of his correspondence, &c. As I am not at all disposed to be either so indulgent, or so correspondent, as they desire, I have but one bad way left to escape the honour they would inflict upon me; and therefore am obliged to desire you would make Dodsley print it immediately (which may be done in less than a week's time) from your copy, but without my name, in what form is most convenient for him, but on his best paper and character; he must correct the press himself, and print it without any interval between the stanzas, because the sense is in some places continued beyond them; and the title must be,—Elegy, written in a Country Churchyard. If he would add a line or two to say it came into his hands by accident, I should like it better. If you behold the Magazine of Magazines in the light that I do, you will not refuse to give yourself this trouble on my account, which you have taken of your own accord before now. If Dodsley do not do this immediately, he may as well let it alone."

The *Elegy* appeared on the 16th of February 1751 in a quarto pamphlet with the following Title-page.

" An Elegy wrote in a Country
Church Yard

London : Printed for R. Dodsley in Pall-Mall ; And sold by M. Cooper in Pater-noster-Row. 1751. [Price Sixpence.]

Advertisement. The following Poem came into my hands by Accident, if the general Approbation with which this little Piece has spread, may be call'd by so slight a Term as Accident. It is this

Approbation which makes it unnecessary for me to make any Apology but to the Author: As he cannot but feel some Satisfaction in having pleas'd so many Readers already, I flatter myself he will forgive my communicating that Pleasure to many more. The Editor."

The Editor is Walpole, as will be seen by Gray's letter *infra.* He pretends to have been one of many readers into whose hands the poem *accidentally* fell, and to have taken the same unwarrantable liberty with it, which had in fact been taken by the Magazine of Magazines. The plain truth might easily have been told as to the circumstances which led to its publication by Dodsley, without any sacrifice of the *anonymity* which Gray desired. And how does a poet indifferent to fame and money prevent the surreptitious publication of his works, by making the public believe that the offence has been *twice* committed with no remonstrance on his part? His real injury is the issue of a bad text; his only remedy the issue of a text revised by himself. Such remedy Macaulay took when an unauthorized edition of his speeches, deformed by ridiculous blunders, was published by Vizetelly. Such remedy Gray did *not* take; with a consequence of which he could not reasonably complain. He writes to Walpole from Cambridge on Ash Wednesday, 1751:

"You have indeed conducted with great decency my little *misfortune;* you have taken a paternal care of it, and expressed much more kindness than could have been expressed [? expected] from so near a relation. But we are all frail; and I hope to do as much for you another time.

Nurse Dodsley has given it a pinch or two in the cradle, that (I doubt) it will bear the marks of as long as it lives. But no matter; we have ourselves suffered under her hands before now; and besides, it will only look the more careless and by *accident* as it were. I thank you for your advertisement, which saves my honour, and in a manner *bien flatteur pour moi*, who should be put to it even to make myself a compliment in good English."

It is hard to understand why Gray's honour needed saving, or how by this expedient it was saved. But the worst of an affectation pushed as far as he pushed it, is that it leads to much bewilderment, and a good deal of superfluous lying.

The 'pinches' administered by 'Nurse' Dodsley were not very severe; the punctuation is perhaps not quite exact; and in stanza 7, l. 3, the word 'they' is twice repeated. There is no interval between the stanzas, but the first line of every stanza is *indented.* Gray took ample pains in the long run that the world should know what he had really written.

To the title of the Pembroke MS. he has appended a note:

"Published in Febry. 1751, by Dodsley: and went thro foui Editions; in two months; and afterwards a fifth, 6th, 7th, and 8th, 9th, and 10th, and 11th. Printed also in 1753 with Mr Bentley's Designs, of wh^{ch} there is a 2nd Edition and again by Dodsley in his Miscellany, Vol. 7th, and in a Scotch Collection called *The Union*, translated into Latin by Chr. Anstey Esq., and the Revd Mr Roberts, and publish'd in 1762; and again the same year by Robert Lloyd, M.A."

The text with the exception of the bracketed stanzas, is given, upon the faith of Mr Gosse, from the edition of Gray's Poems published by Dodsley in 1768.

Mason states that Gray originally gave the poem only "the simple title of 'Stanzas written in a Country Church-yard.' I persuaded him first to call it an Elegy, because the subject authorized him so to do; and the alternate measure, in which it was written, seemed peculiarly fit for that species of composition. I imagined too that so capital a Poem, written in this measure, would as it were appropriate it in future to writings of this sort; and the number of imitations which have since been made of it (even to satiety) seem to prove that my notion was well founded."

Mason delighted to *pose* as Gray's literary *confrère* and adviser; and when we remember that he was capable of inserting in his version of Gray's letters compliments to himself which never came from Gray, we must accept such statements of his, particularly those which refer to this early stage of the friendship between the two men, with great caution.

Johnson was thinking of this sentence of Mason's when (in the Life of Hammond) he said, "Why Hammond *or other writers* have thought the quatrain of ten syllables elegiac it is difficult to tell. The character of the *Elegy* is gentleness and tenuity; but this stanza has been pronounced by Dryden, whose knowledge of English verse was not inconsiderable, to be the most magnificent of all the measures which our language affords.'

Since the name was invented there have been elegies and elegies; but the *residuum* of truth in Johnson's remark is that this measure, because of its stateliness, at once betrays, by mere force of contrast, 'tenuity' of thought. Take one of the three stanzas of Hammond which Johnson derides:

" Panchaia's odours be their costly feast,
        And all the pride of Asia's fragrant year,
    Give them the treasures of the farthest East,
        And what is still more precious, give thy tear."

Even the few weak places of Dryden's *Annus Mirabilis* become through this mould the more obvious. It cannot therefore be successfully employed on trivial themes. It was used *inter alios* by Davenant for his heroic poem of Gondibert; by Hobbes for his curious translation of Homer; by Dryden for his *Annus Mirabilis*. The suggestion that the posthumous publication of Hammond's Love Elegies in 1745 had anything to do with Gray's choice of this measure may be dismissed; it comes oddly from those who affirm that the *Elegy* was begun in 1742.

The Curfew. The evening bell still conventionally called curfew, though the law of the Conqueror, which gave it the name, had long been a dead letter. In Shakespeare the sound of the Curfew is the signal to the spirit-world to be at large. Edgar in *Lear* feigns to recognize 'the foul fiend Flibbertigibbet: he begins at curfew and walks till the first cock' (III. 4. 103); and in *The Tempest*, V. I. 40, the elves 'rejoice to hear the solemn curfew.' The mood of the *Elegy* is that of *Il Penseroso* and the scene in both poems is viewed in the evening twilight:

" Oft on a plat of rising ground
    I hear the far-off curfew sound,
    Over some wide-watered shore,
    Swinging slow with sullen roar."

                                        Milton, *Il Penseroso*, 72—75.

Milton's '*far-off* curfew' reminds us of the squilla *di lontano* of Dante, which Gray quotes for the first line of the *Elegy*. I supply in brackets the rest of the passage; *Purgatorio*, VIII. 1—6.

[Era gia l' ora, che volge 'l disio
A' naviganti, e 'nteneresce 'l cuore
Lo dì ch' han detto a' dolci amici addio:
E che lo nuovo peregrin d' amore
Punge, se ode] squilla *di lontano*
Che paia 'l giorno pianger, che si muore.
[Now was the hour that wakens fond desire
In men at sea, and melts their thoughtful heart
Who in the morn have bid sweet friends farewell,
And pilgrim, newly on his road, with love
Thrills, if he hear] the vesper bell from far
That seems to mourn for the expiring day.   **Cary.**

The curfew tolls from Great S. Mary's, at Cambridge, at 9, from the Curfew Tower of Windsor Castle (nearer the scene of the *Elegy*) at 8, in the evening.

Warton, *Notes on Pope*, vol. I. p. 82, reads:

"The curfew tolls!—the knell of parting day."

But we know exactly what Gray wrote, and what he meant us to read.

2. **wind.** Not *winds*, as so commonly printed.

"'Wind' has a more poetical connotation, for it suggests a long slowly-moving line of cattle rather than a closely packed herd." Phelps.

Add that of Gray's cattle some are returning from the pasture, but others from the plough. Of the innumerable passages that might be quoted in illustration of this line, perhaps that given by Mitford from Petrarch [Pte I. Canzone IV.] is nearest to Gray's picture:

"Veggio, la sera, *i buoi* tornare *sciolti*
Dalle campagne e da' *solcati colli;*"

which, again, is very like Milton's

"what time the labour'd ox
In his loose traces from the furrow came."

Comus, 291, 2.

Cf. also Homer, *Odyssey*, IX. 58:

Ημος δ' ἠέλιος μετενίσσετο βουλυτόνδε.

(when the sun was passing over toward the hour of loosing the oxen).

And Horace's

"Sol ubi montium
mutaret umbras, et juga demeret
bobus fatigatis..."   (*Odes*, III. 6. 42.)

(what time the sun shifted the shadows of the hills and took the yoke from off the laboured oxen).

A scholar-poet could scarcely mention the 'lowing herd' and the 'plowman' without some reminiscence of this old-world note of time.

Cf. also, after Phelps, Ambrose Philips, Pastoral II. *ad fin.*

"And *unyoked* heifers, pacing homeward, low."

4. Cf. after Mitford, Petrarch [Sonetto CLXVIII.]

"Quando 'l sol bagna in mar l' aurato carro
E l' aer nostro e la mia mente imbruna."

"What time the sun
In ocean bathes his golden car and leaves
Over our air—and on my soul—a shade."

Gray's words are more suggestive. In broad daylight the scene

belongs to the toiler; when he withdraws, he resigns it to the solitary
poet, and to the shadows congenial to *his* spirit. Munro renders this
line:

> "Cunctaque dat tenebris, dat potiunda mihi."

6. **And all. And now**—Fraser MS.

Ib. 'Stillness' is here the nominative; 'air' the objective case.

> "aeriumque *tenent otia dia* polum." Munro.

7. **the beetle.** A sinister note of approaching darkness in
Macbeth, III. 2, 42.

> "ere, to black Hecate's summons,
> The *shard-borne beetle with his drowsy hum*
> *Hath rung night's yawning peal*, there shall be done
> A deed of dreadful note."

Dryden (*Absalom and Achitophel*, Pt. I. ll. 301, 2) employs the
beetle to crush

> "such *beetle* things
> As only buzz to heaven with *evening* wings."

In December 1746 Collins published among other poems his *Ode
to Evening*, and Joseph Warton's volume including, I believe, *his*
'Evening' appeared in the same month and year. Collins writes:

> "Now air is hushed save [where the weak-eyed bat
> With short shrill shriek flits by on leathern wing
> Or] where the beetle winds
> His small but sullen horn
> As oft he rises 'midst the twilight path
> Against the pilgrim borne in heedless hum."

And here may be the best place to note after Dr Phelps that the
'whole atmosphere of Collins's *Ode* is similar to that of the *Elegy*. Cf.
especially stanza 10,

> "And hamlets brown, and dim-discovered spires,
> And hears their simple bell, and marks o'er all
> Thy dewy fingers draw
> The gradual dusky veil."'

Dr Phelps notes also that Joseph Warton's verses contain some
of Gray's pictures, and something of the same train of thought: *e.g.*:

> "Hail, meek-eyed maiden, clad in sober grey,
> Whose soft approach the *weary* woodman loves,
> As homeward bent to *kiss his prattling babes*
> Jocund he whistles through the twilight groves."

add :

> "Now every Passion sleeps; desponding Love,
>
> And pining Envy, ever-restless Pride;
>
> *A holy calm* creeps o'er my peaceful soul,
>
> Anger and mad Ambition's storms subside."

The latter stanza might well be the form in embryo of the four rejected stanzas quoted *infra*, n. on l. 72. Dr Phelps remarks that "the scenery as well as the meditations of the *Elegy* were by no means original: they simply established more firmly literary fashions which were already becoming familiar."

And certainly if the opening stanzas of the *Elegy* as we now have them were written as early as 1742, their composition was in no way affected by the poems of Warton and Collins; the same must be said even if the 'autumnal verses' of the letter of Sept. 11, 1746, were the *Elegy*. The spirit of gentle melancholy was in the air; and in 1746 and 1747 found in three young poets, Collins, Joseph Warton and Thomas Warton, that voice to the world at large which is found again in Gray in 1750. For in 1747 Thomas Warton published anonymously these lines, which he had written in his 17th year (1745):

> "Beneath yon ruin'd abbey's moss-grown pile
>
> Oft let me sit, at twilight hour of eve
>
> Where thro' some western window the pale moon
>
> Pours her long-levell'd rule of streaming light;
>
> While sullen *sacred silence* reigns around,
>
> *Save the lone screech-owl's note, who builds his bow'r*
>
> Amid the mould'ring caverns dark and damp,
>
> Or the calm breeze, that rustles in the leaves
>
> *Of flaunting ivy, that with mantle green*
>
> *Invests some wasted tow'r :*"

where resemblance to the *Elegy* is closest of all.

Between these three poets communication of ideas was probable; but at this date even Thomas Warton, with whom he afterwards corresponded, was an absolute stranger to Gray. And Gray is so far from feeling that in any of these there were 'kindred spirits' who might 'enquire his fate' that he writes, Dec. 27, 1746:

'Have you seen the Works of two young Authors, a Mʳ Warton and a Mʳ Collins, both Writers of Odes? it is odd enough, but each is the half of a considerable Man, and one the counterpart of the other. The first has but little invention, very poetical choice of Expression, and a good Ear, the second a fine fancy, model'd upon the Antique, a bad Ear, great variety of Words, and Images with no choice at all. They both deserve to last some Years, but will not.'

So little are men conscious of that 'stream of tendency' on which they themselves are borne.

8. **And.** Or Frazer and Pembroke MSS.; perhaps also Egerton MS.

9. **ivy-mantled tow'r.** The church at Stoke Pogis is undoubtedly most in Gray's mind in the *Elegy*, but we need not suppose that he reproduces his scene like a photographer. If he needed to see an 'ivy-mantled' tower in order to imagine it he would find one at Upton old church, not far from Stoke, but nearer to Slough and Eton.

10. It seems unnecessary to quote from the literature of all ages in illustration of this and like commonplaces of poetry. The skill of Gray lies in the perfect combination of such details;—Thomson and Mallet, almost simultaneously, were enlisting the 'owl'; cf. also Thomas Warton in preceding note. Gray may have remembered the 'ignavus bubo' of Ovid, *Metamorphoses*, v. 550: but we will credit him with sufficient observation to have discovered independently that the owl 'mopes.'

In this picture it is noteworthy that we have a deeper shade of growing nightfall than in the preceding.

11. **bow'r.** The proper sense of bower is any place to be or dwell in; often used in poetry for 'my lady's chamber.' Gray no doubt used the word in its root-sense, but surely with some connotation of 'arbour'; which again is really 'harbour' and has nothing to do with 'arbor,' tree, although the sense 'a *bower made of branches of trees*' points to that as the accepted derivation of the word. Similarly the etymologist Junius thought 'bower' was so called from being made of boughs; a fancy which has no doubt affected the sense of the word.

13. **That yew-tree's shade.** The yew-tree of Gray's time still exists in Stoke Church, according to Dr Bradshaw; 'it is on the south side of the church, its branches spread over a large circumference, and under it, as well as under its shade, there are several graves.'

16. **rude.** Of course in the sense of simple and unlettered.

'The poor people were always buried in the church-yard, the rich inside the church.' Phelps.

17, 18. **For ever sleep: the breezy Call of Morn**
      Or &c.   Fraser MS.

"...Whenas sacred light began to dawn
In Eden, on the humid flowers, that breathed
Their morning incense."

Par. Lost, IX. 193. Wakefield.

19. **Or Chaunticleer so shrill or echoing Horn** Fraser MS.
"...The crested cock, whose *clarion* sounds
The silent hours." *Par. Lost*, VII. 442. Wakefield.
"When chanticleer with *clarion shrill* recalls
The tardy day." J. Philips, *Cyder*, I. 753. Mitford.

Cyder was published in 1708, the year of the death of J. Philips. Philips in the *Splendid Shilling* parodied, and in *Cyder* imitated, Milton. Gray knew his verse well, and perhaps (*Gray and His Friends*, p. 298) at an early date attempted to translate a part of the *Splendid Shilling* into Latin Hexameters.

But here again, if there is imitation at all on Gray's part, it is to be found in the same *combination* of cockcrow and the hunter's horn which Milton had already given in his picture of Morning in *L'Allegro*, l. 49 sq.

"While the cock, with lively din,
Scatters the rear of darkness thin.

. . . .

Oft listening how the hounds and horn
Cheerly rouse the slumbering morn."

20. **lowly bed.** "Lloyd," says Dr Bradshaw, "in his Latin translation strangely mistook 'lowly bed' for the grave."

Dr Phelps on the other hand says, 'This probably refers to the humble couch on which they have spent the night; but it is meant to suggest the grave as well.' This seems probable.

21. **For them** etc.
"Jam jam non domus accipiet te laeta, neque uxor
optima, nec dulces occurrent oscula nati
praeripere et tacita pectus dulcedine tangent."

Lucretius, III. 894—896.

"Now no more shall thy house admit thee with glad welcome, nor a most virtuous wife and sweet children run to be the first to snatch kisses and touch thy heart with a silent joy." (Munro.)

Though Lucretius is only mentioning these common regrets of mankind in order to show their unreasonableness, there is no doubt that Gray had this passage well in his mind here. Feeling this, Munro renders it in quite Lucretian phraseology: *e.g.*

"*Jam jam* non erit his rutilans focus igne:
and
       non reditum balbe current patris *hiscere* nati."
But Gray adds also an Horatian touch, as Mitford points out:
       "Quodsi pudica mulier in partem juvet
              domum atque dulces liberos

              . . . .

           sacrum vetustis excitet lignis focum
           lassi sub adventum viri," &c.   Hor. *Epode*, II. 39 sq.
           ["But if a chaste and pleasing wife
              To ease the business of his life
              Divides with him his household care

              . . . .

              Will fire for winter nights provide,
              And without noise will oversee
              His children and his family
              And order all things till he come
              Weary and over-laboured home" &c.   Dryden.]
Thomson in his *Winter*, 1726, had written of the shepherd over-
whelmed in the snow-storm:
           "In vain for him the officious wife prepares
              The fire fair-blazing, and the vestment warm;
              In vain his little children, peeping out
              Into the mingling rack, demand their sire
              With tears of artless innocence."   (ll. 311—315.)
24. Or. Nor, Fraser MS.

envied. The Fraser MS. has **coming,** with **envied** written above
it, and **doubtful** in the margin. Gray happily decided upon 'envied,'
for 'coming' is a weak word; and 'doubtful' would have been
ambiguous to any but a classical reader,—who alone would feel sure
that the meaning was, it was uncertain to whom the privilege of the
first kiss would fall. Cf. the 'praeripere' of Lucretius *supra*[1].

Cf. Virgil, *Georg.* II. 523 (describing the joys of the husbandman):
       "Interea dulces pendent circum oscula nati."
[Meanwhile sweet children cling round his kisses.   Mackail.]

----

[1] Add Dryden, as quoted by Mitford, (from ed. Warton, vol. ii. p. 565, a futile
reference)

              "Whose little arms around thy legs are cast,
              And climbing for a kiss *prevent* their mother's haste."

25. sickle. Sickles Egerton MS.

26. the stubborn glebe. Luke quotes from Gay's *Fables*, Vol. II. Fable xv. l. 89:

> "'Tis mine to tame the stubborn *glebe.*"

—What Gay really writes is:

> "'Tis mine to tame the stubborn *plain,*
>
> Break the stiff soil, and house the grain."

This is a curious example of the way in which a perfectly needless parallel 'may be made when it cannot be found.'

27. afield, to the field. 'We drove afield,' Milton, *Lycidas*, l. 27; this is probably Gray's warrant for the word. Whether we refer the prefix 'a' to 'on' or to 'at' here, the secondary notion of 'motion towards' is easily attached to it; *e.g.* in Shakespeare 'away' [on way] sometimes means 'hither': and for 'at' in the sense of 'to' cf. '*at* him again!' Instances of 'sturdy stroke' are quoted from Spenser, *Shepherd's Calendar*, February [ll. 201, 202] and, Dryden, *Georgics*, III. 639.

29. useful. Fraser MS. suggests in margin homely; and for homely of next line gives **rustic.**

29—32. "The rimes in this stanza are scarcely exact": says Dr Phelps. That they were at one time exact is certain; and they were probably exact to Gray's time. The wearisome frequency of the rhyme 'join' with such words as 'combine,' 'sign,' 'line,' in Dryden, Pope, &c. establishes the pronunciation of 'join' as 'jine' over a long period up to the middle of the 18th century; in Dryden we have 'spoil' rhyming with 'guile' and 'awhile'; 'boil' rhyming with 'pile,' and in Pope, *Odyssey*, b. I.:

> "Your widow'd heart, apart, with female *toil*
>
> And various labours of the loom *beguile.*"

The very rhyme of the text is doubtless frequent; I find it casually in Johnson's London (**1738**):

> "On all thy hours security shall *smile,*
>
> And bless thine evening walk, and morning *toil.*"

It is on record as an instance of Gray's pronunciation that he would say, 'What *naise* is that?' instead of 'noise.' The sound here indicated must be approximately that of the last syllable of 'recognize'; and analogously it seems probable that Gray himself said 'tile' for 'toil.'

Now for the rhyme of 'obscure' with 'poor.' If Gray pronounced 'scure' much as we pronounce 'skewer,' the rhyme is not quite exact;

but it is more probable, if only from a certain Gallicizing tendency of his, that the sound for him was rather like the French 'obscur.' Dryden's rhyme for 'poor' is most frequently with 'more,' 'store,' &c., from which I infer, doubtfully, that *he* pronounced poor as ' pore.' Pope, makes 'poor' rhyme with 'door' which of itself determines nothing ; but he also makes it rhyme with 'cure,' 'endure' and 'sure'; (which is like Gray) ; and further with 'store' and 'yore' (which is like Dryden). Thus in the famous story of Sir Balaam, with an interval of only two lines we have :

> ... " his gains were *sure,*
> His givings rare, save farthings to the *poor.*

and

> " Satan now is wiser than of *yore,*
> And tempts by making rich, not making *poor.*"

On the whole we may conclude that Gray pronounced 'poor' much as we do, and ' obscure ' so as to rhyme with it.

When such rhymes as this stanza offers became merely conventional it would be harder to determine.

32. *Annals of the Poor*, a pretty book by Leigh Richmond, author also of the *Dairyman's Daughter*, takes its title and motto from this line and stanza, as Dr Bradshaw reminds us.

33—36. Cowley had written:

> " *Beauty* and strength, and wit, and *wealth,* and *power,*
>   Have their short flourishing hour ;
> And love to see themselves, and smile
> And joy in their pre-eminence awhile :
>   E'en so in the same land
> Poor weeds, rich corn, gay flowers together stand.
> Alas ! Death mows down all with an impartial hand."

A passage no doubt known to West, when he wrote, Dec. 1737, in his Monody on the death of Queen Caroline [*Gray and His Friends,* pp. 108, 110—114],

> " Ah me ! what boots us all our boasted power,
>   Our golden treasure, and our purpled state ?
> They cannot ward th' inevitable hour,
>   Nor stay the fearful violence of Fate."

lines which Gray undoubtedly remembers and improves upon here.

35. **Awaits.** The reading 'Await' has no MS. authority ; according to Dr Bradshaw it first appeared in Dodsley's Collection, Vol. IV. published in 1755; but in editions of 1753 and 1768, for the text of

which Gray has some responsibility, we have 'awaits,' as well as in every copy in his handwriting. That 'hour' is the nominative the slightest reflection should show us. We pursue our several ambitions as if unconscious of our doom, it is the hour that awaits *us ;* if *we* awaited the hour we should be less absorbed in our aims. The sentiment of the stanza is Horatian ; omnes una manet nox—one night awaits us all, says Horace in the 28th Ode of the 1st Book ; he has spoken of philosophers, Archytas, Pythagoras; heroes, Tantalus, Tithonus, Minos, Euphorbus, and proceeds to tell us how the warrior perishes in battle, and the sailor in the sea :

> "Dant alios Furiae torvo spectacula Marti :
>
> Exitio est avidum mare nautis," &c.

Conington translates, unluckily perpetuating the misreading in the *Elegy,* but acknowledging the identity of thought :

> "Yes, all 'await the inevitable hour' ;
>
> The downward journey all one day must tread,
>
> Some bleed to glut the war-gods' savage eyes ;
>
> Fate meets the sailor from the hungry brine ;
>
> Youth jostles age in funeral obsequies ;
>
> Each brow in turn is touched by Proserpine."

The paths. Here again there is the frequent misquotation ' The path of glory *leads,*' &c. Gray means, after Horace, that whatever way to fame we select, the end is the same. Accordingly Munro renders this line :

> "metaque mors, *quoquo* gloria flectit iter."

36. In Kippis, *Biographia Britannica,* Vol. IV. p. 429, in the *Life of Crashaw,* written by Hayley, it is said that this line is "literally translated from the Latin prose of Bartholinus in his Danish Antiquities." Mitford.

Nothing accessible to me shows that Gray was at all acquainted with Bartholin at the date of the completed *Elegy* (see introduction and notes to *Norse Odes, infra*).

37. **Forgive ye proud th' involuntary Fault**
If Memory to these &c.

Fraser and according to Bradshaw all MSS. Bradshaw adds 'The present reading is written in the margin ' ; but I did not find this so in Fraser MS.

39. **isle.** Spelt **Ile** by Gray, in Fraser MS. The word is from French *aile,* a wing, and the s, says Skeat, is a meaningless insertion.

fretted. A fret is defined by Bloxham, *Glossary of Architecture,* 'an ornament used in Classical architecture, formed by small fillets intersecting each other at right angles'; a fillet, again, is a narrow band used principally between mouldings, both in Classical and Gothic architecture. It is Gothic architecture that Gray has in his mind's eye ; the lines that go to make the fanshaped roof of King's College Chapel or of S. George's, Windsor, for example.

The derivation of 'fret,' 'fretted,' in this technical sense is uncertain. Skeat hesitates between tracing it to an A.-S. word meaning to 'adorn,' or through French and Low-Latin to 'ferrum.' In Heraldry fret means 'a bearing composed of bars crossed and interlaced,' and for this sense of the word Skeat suggests the latter, not the A.-S. derivation. Littré, however, traces the heraldic term to the same origin as *flèche*, an arrow.

It seems probable that the architectural and heraldic word, representing much the same sort of device, are one and the same, and have a common origin, whatever that may be.

Note Shakespeare's use of the word :

> *Dec.* Here lies the east: doth not the day break here ?
> *Casca.* No.
> *Cinna.* O pardon, sir, it doth ; and yon grey lines
> That *fret the clouds* are messengers of day.
> > *Jul. Caes.* (II. 1, 104).

—lines of light that shoot athwart the clouds and intersect them.

But *Hamlet*, II. 2, 313, 'this majestical roof fretted with golden fire' is less clear. For these frets may be 'Hyperion's *shafts*' or 'fretted' may mean 'studded' or 'embossed' with stars, the 'stellèd fires' of which he speaks in *Lear*. The word proper to the long lines that mark out the roof may be applied to the ornaments in which such lines might terminate or be concentred,—so in *Cymbeline*, II. 4. 88:

> "The roof o' the chamber
> With *golden cherubins* is *fretted*."

Perhaps Munro would interpret Gray's 'fretted' in the sense of 'embossed' for he renders this line :

> "longus ubi alarum ductus, *crustataque* fornix"

where, I think, by 'crustata' he means set with decorations moulded in plaster or the like pliable material.

vault. 'The high embowèd roof' of Milton, *Il Penseroso*, 157.

41. An urn with an inscription on it, a common form of funereal monument in imitation more or less of the antique. The 'pictured urn'

of *Progress of Poesy*, l. 109, which Dr Bradshaw here compares is quite a different thing.

Animated bust. Cf. Pope, *Temple of Fame*, ll. 73, 74:

> "Heroes in animated marble frown,
>   And legislators seem to think in stone."

But the original both for Gray and Pope is Virgil, *Aen.* VI. 848, 849:

> "Excudent alii *spirantia* mollius aera,
>   Credo equidem; *vivos* ducent de *marmore vultus*."

'Others shall beat out the breathing bronze to softer lines; I believe it well; shall draw *living* lineaments from the marble.' (Mackail.)

Cf. *Georg.* III. 34:

> "Stabunt et Parii lapides, *spirantia* signa."

[' There too shall stand *breathing* images in Parian stone.' *Id.*]

The expression is rescued from the charge of imitation or conventionalism by the thought which it is made to serve, that all the skill of the artist in simulating the breath of life cannot bring it ' back to its mansion.'

43. **provoke.** Call to life, rouse to action, a classical use of the word, as in Pope, *Ode on St Cecilia's Day*, III.

> "But when our country's cause *provokes* to arms."

In Fraser MS. Gray writes '**awake**' in the text, suggesting '**provoke**' in the margin. The alteration is a clue to the meaning he attaches 'to honour's voice,' which Dr Bradshaw interprets to be ' words or speeches in honour of the dead.' This does not give the right significance to 'honour' here. Among the ' paths of glory,' lineage, statecraft, beauty, wealth, are named (33—36); it would be strange if the poet made no reference to the calling with which 'glory' is most associated. He has the 'brave' here specially in mind; of whose tombs Collins writes:

> "There *honour* comes, a pilgrim gray,
>   To bless the turf that wraps their clay."

Honour, whose servants they were, may bless or praise them: but they can no longer rise at that voice which in life they were so eager to obey. To this effect Munro's version:

> "Voce valet cinerem succendere *gloria* mutum."

44. **dull, cold.** They compare Wolsey, in *Henry VIII.* III. 2. 434:

> "And when I am forgotten, as I shall be,
>   And sleep in *dull cold* marble."

46. **pregnant...fire]** Cowper has the expression in *Boadicea*:

> "Such the bard's prophetic words,
>> *Pregnant with celestial fire,*
>
> Bending as he swept the chords
>
> Of his sweet but awful lyre." Bradshaw.

47. Mitford quotes Ovid [*Heroides*] Ep. v. l. 86 [Œnone Paridi.]

"Sunt mihi quas possint sceptra decere manus."

Fraser MS. reads '**reins** of empire' here. Dr Bradshaw suggests that Gray made the alteration because Tickell (cited by Mitford) had written, *Poem to Earl of Warwick*, l. 37:

"Proud names that once *the reins of empire* held."

48. **Wake to ecstasy.** Cf. *Progress of Poetry*, l. 2. Mitford quotes from Cowley, without reference:

"Begin the song and strike *the living lyre*."

Pope no doubt had this line in mind when he wrote in *Windsor Forest*, l. 281 (cited by Mitford):

"Who now shall charm the shades, where Cowley strung

His *living harp*, and lofty Denham sung?"

49. The germ of the four following stanzas is probably to be found in these lines of Waller (to Zelinda):

> "Great Julius on the mountains bred,
>
> A flock perhaps or herd had led,
>
> He that the world subdued had been
>
> But the best wrestler on the green.
>
> 'Tis art and knowledge which draw forth
>
> The hidden seeds of native worth;
>
> They blow those sparks and make them rise
>
> Into such flames as touch the skies."

Gray possessed and had studied Waller; he has transferred this thought from a trivial setting, and placed it where it fitly exemplifies the pathos of human life.

It should be noted that Gray's Cromwell was originally Caesar, Waller's 'Great Julius.'

49. **Rich with the spoils of time.** Mitford compares Sir T. Browne, *Religio Medici* [Pt. 1. Sect. XIII. where he breaks into verse],

> "And then at last, when homeward I shall drive,
>> *Rich with the spoils of nature*, to my hive,
>
> There will I sit, like that industrious fly
>
> Buzzing thy praises" &c.

Whether Gray needed this quaint original to inspire him may be questioned.

unroll. The word, as Bradshaw points out, is suggested by the primary meaning of *volumen* when used of a book, i.e. a scroll, unrolled in order to be read.

51. **rage,** ardent ambition. Gray is thinking of possible statesmen and warriors, as well as poets; although it is of poetic inspiration that the word was commonly used in a good sense. Mitford quotes Pope to Jervas (the painter), l. 12:

" Like them [Dryden and Fresnoy] to shine through long suc-
        ceeding age,
    So just thy skill, so *regular my rage*,"

where the epithet 'regular,' so singularly inept for that which is by its very nature without restraint, shows that this conventional use of 'rage' is really a misuse of it. It is employed, oddly enough, in connection with a reed, by Collins (1746) of Music in *Ode on the Passions* (quoted by Bradshaw):

        " 'Tis said, and I believe the tale,
            Thy humblest *reed* could more prevail,
            Had more of strength, diviner *rage*,
            Than all which charms this laggard age."

But the word scarcely in this use of it belongs to our best poetic diction, for example Shakespeare employs it thus only once, and then with a clear notion of exaggeration (Sonnet XVII. 11);

" The age to come would say, ' This poet lies':
    So should my papers, yellowed with their age,
    Be scorn'd, like old men of less truth than tongue,
    And your true rights be termed a poet's *rage*
    And stretchèd metre of an antique song."

The word indeed belongs to what Johnson calls ' the contortions of the Sibyll':

        "et *rabie* fera corda tument." *Aen.* VI. 49.

from which, and the kindred inspiration of the Pythoness, the expression has been transferred to a milder enthusiasm; Shakespeare is nearest to adopting it when he speaks of ' the poet's eye in a fine *frenzy* rolling.' Milton never uses it in this way at all.

52. **genial.** The word connotes at once cheering and fertilising; the fervour and the creative power of genius. Its two senses in Latin are ' belonging to generation or birth' and ' belonging to enjoyment,

jovial.' Gray has used it in the double sense of 'kindly' and 'pro-
ductive' in *Alliance of Education and Government*, l. 3:

"Nor *genial* warmth, nor *genial* juice retains,
    Their roots to feed, and fill their verdant veins."

Ib. Cf. Scott's *Old Mortality*, chap. XIII. where with obvious reminiscence of this stanza, it is said of Henry Morton, 'the *current of his
soul was frozen* by a sense of dependence—of *poverty*—above all, *of
an imperfect and limited education*.'

53, 54. Mitford cites Milton, *Comus*, 22:

"That like to rich and various gems inlay
    The unadornèd bosom of the deep;"

but, very inappositely, since the 'sea-girt isles' to which the simile
refers are conspicuous and on the surface, whilst it is of the essence
of Gray's thought that the gems are invisible and at the bottom.
Milton's thought is in fact Shakespeare's (*Rich. II.* II. 1. 46):

"This precious stone, set in the silver sea."

The quotation from Bishop Hall's *Contemplations*, VI. 872, is
better: "There is many a rich stone laid up in the bowells of the
earth, many a fair *pearle in the bosome of the sea*, that never was seene
nor never shall bee." Noteworthy perhaps as a coincidence is the
line Mitford quotes from the Greek of an Italian poet (I think), of
the *Renaissance*:

Μάργαρα πολλὰ βαθὺς συγκρύπτει κύμασι πόντος,

[Many a pearl far under the waves lies hidden of Ocean.]

55. Mitford gives these parallels (the exact references are due
to Dr Phelps):

William Chamberlayne, *Pharonnida* (London, 1659, Book IV.
canto 5, p. 94):

"Like beauteous flowers which vainly waste the scent
    Of odors in unhaunted deserts."

From Ambrose Philips (1671—1749] *The Fable of Thule:*

"Like beauteous flowers, which paint the desert glades,
    And waste their sweets in unfrequented shades."

From Young, *Universal Passion* [1725], Sat. V. ll. 229—232 :

"In distant wilds, by human eyes unseen
    She rears her flow'rs, and spreads her velvet green.
    Pure gurgling rills the lonely desert trace
    And waste their music on the savage race."

Mr Yardley in *Notes and Queries* (Sept. 1, 1894) suggests that Gray
imitated Waller's 'Go, lovely Rose':

> "Tell her that's young
> And shuns to have her graces spied
> That, hadst thou sprung
> In deserts where no men abide,
> Thou must have uncommended died."

Perhaps this is the starting-point in the line of succession of the poetical idea for Gray: but it passes through Pope and comes nearer in the form:

> "There kept my charms concealed from mortal eye,
> Like roses that in deserts bloom and die."

Rape of the Lock, IV. 157, 158.

This idea Pope cherished, for he gave it, in an improved form, to Thomson for the *Seasons*: the lines in the episode of Lavinia, Autumn, 209—214,

> "As in the hollow breast of Apennine,
> Beneath the shelter of encircling hills,
> A myrtle rises, far from human eye,
> And breathes its balmy fragrance o'er the hills,
> So flourished blooming, and unseen by all,
> The sweet Lavinia."

are to be seen, in a handwriting, probably Pope's, in an interleaved copy of the *Seasons* (ed. 1738) in the British Museum [C 28 E.] Whether Gray had seen these lines, not published until 1744, will depend upon the date we assign to this portion of the *Elegy*.

56. **desert air.** Wakefield compares Pindar, *Ol.* I. 10, ἐρήμας δι᾽ αἰθέρος; and Rogers, *Macbeth,* IV. 3. 194,

> "I have words
> That would be howl'd out into the *desert air.*"

This line, as the present editor pointed out to Dr Bradshaw, soon became proverbial. It is found in Churchill's *Gotham,* 1764:

> "So that they neither give a tawdry glare
> Nor 'waste their sweetness on the desert air.'"

57 sq. **Hampden,** &c. The line in Fraser MS. stands thus:
Some village Cato   with dauntless Breast.
the missing word is, I suppose, either now invisible or was never written. (I have only seen the facsimile.)

Why did Gray select *Cato?* I think (and this tends to confirm my notion that his original was Waller) it was because in the order of his thoughts, though not of his setting of them, he began with Caesar. This suggests Cato of Utica, and his resistance to Caesar's

T. G.   4 tyranny. Otherwise the withstander of the 'tyrant of the fields' might well have found his greater counterpart in Gracchus, as the champion of the fast dwindling class of small landed proprietors against the large landowners of Italy. It is both for this reason, and because Cato, a true oligarch and the opponent of the popular party in Rome, was no fitting analogue to Hampden that Munro in translating this line, instead of reverting to Gray's original hero, writes:

> "forsitan hic olim intrepido qui pectore ruris
> restiterat parvo *Graccus agrestis* ero
> vel mutus sine honore Maro, vel Julius alter
> immunis patrii sanguinis ille, cubet."

Of course Virgil was inevitable as the counterpart to Milton. But note that both in Gray's first conception and in his second his types are all contemporary; Caesar, Cato, Cicero suggested one another irresistibly to his student-mind, and it must not be forgotten that the debates on the Catilinarian conspiracy bring precisely these three names into prominence in the pages of Sallust. When he changed his *terrain* Gray again sought and found contemporaries; with the additional link in common that Hampden, Milton, Cromwell, were all associated in the same cause, and all, in some sense, champions of liberty.

By a happy coincidence the English examples which Gray substituted for the Roman had all some connection with the neighbourhood of Gray's churchyard. It was at Horton, which is at no great distance from Stoke Pogis, that Milton in his younger days composed *L'Allegro, Il Penseroso, Arcades, Comus, Lycidas;* it was to Chalfont St Giles within a few miles of the churchyard that in his old age he retired from the Great Plague of London with the finished MS. of *Paradise Lost.* Hampden was a Buckinghamshire squire, his family seat was Great Hampden, in the hundred of Aylesbury, he represented first Wendover, and then the county in Parliament. Cromwell was his cousin, and often visited both Hampden and his sister, Mrs Waller (the mother of the poet), who lived at Beaconsfield[1].

---

[1] "Waller's mother, though related to Cromwell and Hampden, was zealous for the royal cause, and when Cromwell visited her used to reproach him; he in return would throw a napkin at her, and say he would not dispute with his aunt [i.e. cousin]: but finding in time that she acted for the king as well as talked he made her a prisoner to her own daughter, in her own house." Johnson's Waller in *Lives of the Poets.*

Mitford records a line of Gray's in pencil:
The rude Columbus of an infant world.
This is possibly an afterthought for another stanza (of which it might have formed the first line), pointing to other lines of enterprise in embryo.

We lack a context by which to determine the sense of ' an *infant* world,' which may be used much as Berkeley writes of ' happy climes the seat of innocence,' or of ' Time's noblest *offspring*' as 'the *last*.' But on more general grounds we may safely conjecture that Gray had some thought of developing amid humbler scenes the picture sketched in the Eton Ode of those ' bold adventurers '

> " who disdain
> The limits of their little reign
> And unknown regions dare descry."

One thinks of Wordsworth's *Blind Highland Boy*, who had heard how, in a tortoise-shell,

> " An English boy, oh thought of bliss !
> Had stoutly launch'd from shore,"

and was tempted to follow his example.

58. **fields. lands,** erased in MS. (Fraser). So Mitford records. This, if it is so, escaped my notice.

59. **Milton. Tully** Fraser M.

60. **Cromwell. Caesar** Fraser MS. ' See Cromwell damned to everlasting fame," Pope, *Essay on Man*, IV. 284. Mark Pattison observes of Pope, that ' in estimating historical characters he seems to have been without any proper standard, and wholly at the mercy of prevailing social prejudices.' But the prejudice against Cromwell in the eighteenth century was shared by men of very various opinions; literature in the *seventeenth* century was, on its lower levels, more vituperative, but on its higher, more appreciative and generous; the tributes of Milton and Marvell to Cromwell were of course spontaneous, but even those of Waller and Dryden were not altogether forced; they have a certain ring of sincerity about them. It is in the main Carlyle who has *rehabilitated* Cromwell in the popular mind.

61. Pope, *Moral Essays*, I. 184 (speaking of Wharton). ' Though wondering senates hung on all he spoke.' Mitford.

62. As Sir Thomas More, Sir John Eliot, Hampden, Algernon Sidney, Lord William Russell—heroes commemorated in Thomson's *Summer*, ll. 1488—1530; More as a ' dauntless soul erect, who smiled on death,' and Sidney as the British Cassius who ' fearless bled.'

63. Bradshaw compares *Education and Government*, ll. **17**, 18, where it is the attribute of Justice to

> "Scatter with a free, though frugal, hand
>   Light golden showers of plenty o'er the land."

65. lot. Fate in Fraser MS. with **lot** written over it.

65, 66. 'circumscrib'd' and 'confin'd' are finite verbs, the nominative being 'lot.'

66. growing. struggling in Fraser MS. with **growing** written over it.

67. Wakefield compares Pope's *Temple of Fame*, l. **347**, where heroes addressing the goddess say:

> "[For thee...amidst alarms and strife
>   We sailed in tempests down the stream of life;]
>   For thee whole nations fill'd with flames and blood,
>   And swam to empire through the purple flood."

68. And. Or Egerton MS.

Henry V. III. 3. **10.** 'The gates of mercy shall be all shut up.' Mitford.

69—72. The general sense of the stanza seems to be: Their lot forbade them to be eminent persecutors (l. **69**), unscrupulous place-hunters, or ministers to vice in high places (l. **70**), or courtly and venal poets (ll. **71, 72**).

69. The struggleing-s pangs, &c. Fraser MS. showing that Gray had some thought of making 'struggleing' a trisyllabic substantive, and changed his mind. He spells the same word without e in l. 66 (note) when it is a dissyllable.

71, 72. Thus in Fraser MS:

> **And at the Shrine of Luxury and Pride**
>
> **With Incense hallowed ^{by} the Muse's Flame.**
> **Burn   in**

This shows that Gray had some intention at one time to continue the sense into a following stanza.

71. Shrine. Shrines Egerton MS.

72. After this follows in Fraser MS.,

> "The thoughtless World to Majesty may bow
>   Exalt the brave, and idolize Success
>   But more to Innocence their Safety owe
>   Than Power and Genius e'er conspired to bless
>   And thou, who mindful of the unhonour'd Dead
>   eir
>   Dost in these Notes thy artless Tale relate

> By Night and lonely Contemplation led
> To linger in the gloomy walks of Fate
>   Hark how the sacred Calm, that broods around
> Bids ev'ry fierce tumultuous Passion cease
> In still small Accents whisp'ring from the Ground
> A grateful Earnest of eternal Peace
>   No more with Reason and thyself at Strife
> Give anxious Cares and endless Wishes room
> But thro the cool sequester'd Vale of Life
> Pursue the silent Tenour of thy Doom"

"And here," says Mason, "the poem was originally intended to conclude, before the happy idea of 'the hoary-headed Swain &c.' suggested itself to him."

Mason perhaps converted Walpole by a reference to the state of this MS., which no doubt establishes an interval between the first and second half of the poem. But he ante-dated, it may be suspected, the composition of the first half.

The Fraser MS. (to judge from the facsimile) has a line drawn along the side of the last three, and possibly meant (as Sir W. Fraser's reprint interprets it) to include the first also of these four, stanzas.

The stanzas which follow these four are:

Far from the madding crowd's &c.

as in the received text (with minor variations to be noted), down to 'fires,' l. 92.

All the MS. to the end of the four rejected Stanzas is in a much more faded character; and Mason must be at least so far right that the Poem from 'Far from the madding &c.' was resumed after a considerable interval.

But we have only Mason's authority for the statement that the *Elegy* was ever meant to end with these four stanzas, and it is very questionable. We may be biased by the completeness of the poem in its published form,—but surely without this contrast to assist our judgment it would have seemed to us to finish baldly and abruptly with

"Pursue the silent Tenour of thy Doom."

And if this ending would not satisfy us it could not have satisfied Gray. Again, it is probable from the MS. that down to 'Doom' the *Elegy* was all written much about the same time, or as the Germans say, *in einem Guss.* Suppose then it had reached that point in 1742, and this is probably what Mason means when he suggests that it may have been concluded then; is it conceivable that Gray, who had

communicated to Walpole other completed poems of that date, and
even the fragmentary *Agrippina*, would have kept back the *Elegy*,
which *ex hypothesi* he must have regarded as finished? Yet Walpole,
as we have seen, is certain that Gray sent him only the first three
stanzas, two or three years after the year 1742. Surely either these
twelve lines were all that Gray had then written, or they were a
specimen only of the unfinished poem.

73.   **Far from the madding Crowd's ignoble strife;**
In Fraser MS., the punctuation showing that it was the poet's
first intention to make the line part of the *apostrophe* to himself. It
echoes the sentiment of Gray's beautiful Alcaic Ode written in the
album of the Grande Chartreuse Aug. 1741, as he was returning from
his sojourn in Italy, in which he says,—if he cannot have the silence of
the cloistered cell:—

> Saltem remoto des, Pater, angulo
> Horas senectae ducere liberas
>   Tutumque *vulgari tumultu*
>   Surripias, *hominumque curis.*

> At least, O Father, ere the close of life
>   Vouchsafe, I pray thee, some sequestered glen,
> And there seclude me, rescued from the strife
>   Of vulgar tumults and the cares of men.

> [R. E. Warburton in *Notes and Queries*, June 9, 1883.]

Mason is perhaps so far right that it was with this *wish* that the
Elegy, like the Alcaic Ode was meant to end; we may admit this
without supposing that it was intended to close with 'Doom.'

But whilst it is probable, from the punctuation of 'strife,' that Gray
meant through this and possibly other stanzas to end the *Elegy* after the
manner of the Alcaic Ode, it is quite clear that he soon abandoned that
intention; for 'strife' here necessitated in the ending of the first line of
previous stanza:

'No more with reason and thyself at *strife*,'—
and in the corresponding rhyme, some alteration which he never took
the trouble to make, preferring to give his thoughts a more general
scope and to use the four stanzas above cited as far only as they could
be set in a natural sequence on this new model. This is the explanation
of his side line. He in fact could avail himself only of two stanzas, the
second and the fourth; the first 'The thoughtless World' &c. has in
either sequence a little too much the character of a detached sentiment
to please him, and, upon the altered plan, it was, for the same reason,

difficult to introduce the third. We may well regret this, for Mason is right in saying that it is equal to any in the whole *Elegy*.

'Far from the Madding Crowd' is the title of one of Thomas Hardy's best novels, in which every one of the characters is drawn from humble life.

madding. 'Far from the madding worldling's harsh discords' Drummond, cited by Rogers. Once, as Bradshaw notes, in Milton, *P. L.* VI. 210:

> "[arms on armour clashing brayed
>   Horrible discord, and] the madding wheels
>   Of brazen chariots raged."

Gray himself in *Agrippina*, l. 83: 'the madding ear of rage.'

It may be questioned whether either Drummond or Gray used the word exactly in the sense of 'maddening.' It seems with them to mean 'frenzied.'

'If there were no comma after "strife," the sense of this couplet would be precisely the opposite of what Gray intended.' Phelps.

Even with the comma, there is some carelessness in employing the word 'stray' so close upon 'far from' &c. &c. with which there is a natural temptation to connect it. It is not in perfect lucidity of expression that Gray shines. It may be that he was disposed to retain the semicolon after 'strife' (vide *supra*) as avoiding the ambiguity, which is traceable in part to Gray's change of mind.

76. **noiseless**. 'silent' in Fraser MS., with 'noiseless' written over it.

77 sq. "The four stanzas, beginning 'Yet even these bones,' are to me original: I have never seen the notions in any other place: yet he that reads them here persuades himself that he has always felt them." Johnson (cf. Boswell's *Johnson*, 1775, ætat. 66).

Johnson's comment well illustrates Pope's line in the *Essay on Criticism*:

'What oft was thought but ne'er so well expressed'

which gives us briefly the aim and achievement of the best 18th century poetry.

78. **still**. Both Dr Bradshaw and Dr Phelps explain 'still' as 'always,' Dr Phelps adds 'as commonly in Shakespeare.' I question this explanation, which is only encouraged by the absence of the comma, and I cannot agree with Dr Phelps that Gray was particular about his punctuation; from my experience of his otherwise most carefully written MSS., I should say that he sometimes errs by excess

and sometimes by defect in this. It is surely more natural to suppose that he means 'though they have no stately tombs, and though their lives were most obscure, there remains some frail memorial of them still, in the gravestones around, to plead that they may not be quite forgotten.' Is it true that every grave in a country churchyard has had its stone and its inscription at some time or other?

81. **spelt...muse.** 'Under the yew tree [in the churchyard at Stoke] there is a tombstone with several words wrongly spelt, and some letters ill-formed, and even in the inscription which Gray composed for his aunt's tomb, the word "resurrection" is spelt incorrectly by the unlettered stone-cutter.' Bradshaw.

82. **elegy. epitaph** Fraser MS. The change is a distinct improvement, for the rustic inscriptions *are* epitaphs, however rude.

84. **That teach.** Mitford writes in second *Life of Gray*, "As this construction is not, as it now stands, correct, I think that Gray originally wrote '*to teach*' but altered it afterwards, *euphoniae gratia*, and made the grammar give way to the sound." That euphony was Gray's motive is probable, but the Fraser MS. shows that it was his motive from the first; there is no such *alteration* there, as Mitford supposes.

83 sq. Here again want of lucidity is the one defect in a beautiful stanza. Gray *seems* to mean 'who ever was so much a prey to dumb Forgetfulness as to resign life and its possibilities of joy and sorrow without some regret?' But not only is it patent that millions have been so much a prey to the 'second childishness and mere oblivion' of age that they have passed away without the power to feel regret, but the whole sequence of thought shows that this cannot be Gray's meaning. He uses 'prey' in a prospective sense, the *destined* prey; accordingly Munro translates

Quis *subiturus* enim Lethaea silentia &c.

It is perhaps Gray's classicism which betrays him here, for Horace, who has sometimes the same sort of obscurity due to condensation, has just this anticipatory use when he says (*Odes*, II. 3. 21 sq.) that it makes no difference whether as rich and high-born or poor and low-born you linger out life's little day, *the victim of merciless Orcus*; i.e. certain in either case to become so at last.

Again, Gray seems to be shaping anew the question in *Paradise Lost* (II. 146 sq.):

"For who would lose,
Though full of pain, this intellectual being,

> These thoughts that wander through eternity,
> To perish rather, swallowed up and lost
> In the wide womb of uncreated Night,
> Devoid of sense and motion?"

and when he speaks of 'this pleasing anxious being' and 'the warm precincts of the cheerful day,' he may be supposed to express the same horror of the annihilation of thought, the same dread of eternal darkness. Yet, in the main, the terror of which Gray speaks is the forgetfulness of the dead by the living. In this and the following stanza the true significance of the 'frail memorials' is explained. Though men are destined to oblivion they crave to be remembered, as they have craved for human support and affection in their last hours; it is thus that 'even from the tomb the voice of nature cries.' In fact whilst we find the form and some of the accessories of Gray's thought in Milton, we find the substance of it rather in Homer, Virgil and Dante, who give us the same voice of nature as heard from the further shore; as when the spirits say to Dante, *Inferno*, XVI. 85 sq.:

> "if thou escape this darksome clime
> Returning to behold the radiant stars,
> *See that of us thou speak amongst mankind.*"

84. **pleasing anxious.** Milton's 'intellectual being,' delightful in spite of pain and trouble. Grammarians call this figure *oxymoron*, something which is the more pointed because it seems paradoxical. It abounds in Shakespeare. Munro here renders

> " *dulce*
>
> *tormentum* hanc animam &c."

85. Correspondingly, in Homer, Virgil, Dante, the *desiderium* of the departed is for the *light* of the upper air.

precincts. Gray probably took this expression from *Paradise Lost*, III. 88, the only place in Milton's poems where 'precincts' occurs:

> 'Not far off Heaven in the precincts of light.' Bradshaw.

Note that Milton accentuates the word on the last syllable, Gray, in modern fashion, on the first.

89. So Drayton in his *Moses*, p. 1564, vol. IV. ed. 1753:

> "It is some comfort to a wretch to die,
>
> (If there be comfort in the way of death)
>
> To have some friend, or kind alliance by
>
> To be officious at the parting breath." Mitford.

'It has been suggested that the first line of Gray's stanza seems to regard the near approach of death; the second its actual advent; the third, the time immediately succeeding its advent; the fourth, a time still later.' Bradshaw.

For a like sequence of moments cf. n. on the third stanza.

91. Some lines in the *Anthologia Latina*, p. 680, Ep. CLIII. have ı strong resemblance to those in the text:

> " Crede mihi, vires aliquas natura sepulchris
>   Adtribuit, tumulos vindicat umbra suos."

See also Ausonius (*Parentalia*), ed. Tollii, p. 109:

> " Gaudent compositi cineres sua nomina dici."   Mitford.

(The quotation from Ausonius may illustrate also v. 81.)

92. Gray himself quotes here in illustration:

> " Ch'i veggio nel pensier, dolce mio fuoco,
>   Fredda una lingua, e due begli occhi chiusi
>   Rimaner dopo noi pien di faville."

Petrarch, *Son*. CLXIX. CLI.

He had already, I believe, made the translation of this sonnet, which is preserved among his Latin poems; perhaps even the turn which he has given to it in the lines

> "Nos duo cumque erimus parvus uterque cinis,"

and

> " Ardebitque urnâ multa favilla meâ,"

may have set him on embodying in this place of the *Elegy* the passage quoted. Petrarch's words serve Gray's purpose best if severed from their context. In this sonnet the poet plays with the image of *flame*. He is burning; all believe this, save her whom alone he wishes to believe it; his ardour, of which she makes no account, and the glory he has given her in his rhyme, may yet inflame a thousand others:

> "For in my thought I see,—sweet fire of mine!—
>   A tongue though chilled, and two fair eyes, though sealed,
>   Fraught with immortal sparks, survive us still."

Mitford quotes Chaucer, *Cant. Tales*, Reeve's prologue (3880):

> " Yet in our ashen cold is fire yreken."

But the Reeve is speaking of the passions of youth surviving in old age.

And buried Ashes glow with Social Fires. Fraser MS.

And in our Ashes glow their wonted Fires. Egerton and Pembroke MS.

Awake and faithful to her wonted Fires. 1st and 2nd editions.

93. **For thee.** In Fraser MS. Gray thus writes:

> '**For Thee, who mindful** &c.: as above.'

He meant to bring in the second of the four rejected stanzas, followed by this, (Frazer MS.):

> **If chance that e'er some pensive Spirit more,**
> **By sympathetic Musings here delay'd**
> **With vain, tho' kind, Enquiry shall explore**
> **Thy once-loved Haunt, this long-deserted Shade.**
> **Haply** &c.

95. **If chance.** Shakespeare certainly seems to use 'chance' as a verb in such instances as 'How *chance* thou art returned so soon?' (*Com. of Errors* I. 2. 42), and *Lear* II. 3. 62 'How chance the King comes with so small a train?' Yet it is probable that 'if chance' is 'if perchance,' the substantive used adverbially. Cf. the similar use of 'if case.' ('Case' is not, I think, found as a verb.) 'If case some one of you would fly from us' (3 *Henry* VI. v. 4. 34; and ('to a Painted Lady' a poem doubtfully attributed to Donne), 'But case there be a difference in the mould' &c. (*in* case, probably).

97. **may. shall** Fraser MS.

98. Bradshaw compares Milton, *Comus* 138 sq.:

> " Ere the blabbing eastern scout
> The nice Morn, on the Indian steep
> From her cabined loophole *peep*."

And in the *Installation Ode* (where the words are assigned to Milton, with the same rhyme as here):

> "Oft at the blush of dawn
> I trod your level lawn." ll. 30, 31.

99, 100. Milton's words again:

> " ...though from off the boughs each morn
> We brush mellifluous dews."
> *Par. Lost* v. 428, 429.

> "Together both, ere the high *lawns* appeared
> Under the opening eyelids of the morn
> We drove afield." *Lycidas* 25–27. Bradshaw.

> **With hasty Footsteps brush the Dews away**
> **On the high Brow of yonder hanging Lawn.**
> Fraser MS.

100. Gray, as Mitford suggests, may be influenced by the phrase 'incontro al sol' as used by Petrarch and Tasso in a similar connection.

101–104. "I rather wonder that he rejected this stanza, as it not only has the same sort of Doric delicacy, which charms us peculiarly in this part of the Poem, but also compleats the account of his whole day: whereas, this Evening scene being omitted, we have only his Morning walk, and his Noon-tide repose." Mason.

The stanza is here replaced in brackets, although it is conceivable that Gray may have rejected it, because, though the day is completed by it, it is not completed in sequence. But he might easily have achieved the exact sequence if he had written the rejected lines after ll. 105–108 instead of before them. As Dr Bradshaw points out, in ll. 113, 114, the custom'd *hill*, the *heath*, and *his fav'rite tree*, have obvious reference to the *three* scenes which the youth was known to haunt; so again have the *rill*, the *lawn* and the *wood* on ll. 115, 116. But, if the bracket should be removed, it is indispensable that we should return to the reading 'With gestures quaint' (l. 109) of Fraser MS. For it is obvious that Gray wrote 'Hard by yon wood' instead of it, when he had made up his mind to excise this stanza, yet saw that ll. 115, 116 implied a previous mention of three scenes.

103.   Cf. the impromptu couplet preserved by Norton Nicholls, p. 75 *supra*.

104.   **Whistful** *sic* in Fraser MS. It is possible that this spelling represents some vague etymological notion on Gray's part (though he could scarcely have connected the word with 'whist' in the sense of silent), and shows at any rate that he did not derive it from 'wist' in the sense either of 'knew' or 'known'—which derivation, says Skeat, 'is stark nonsense.' Skeat believes that *wistful* stands for *wishful*, the change in form being due to confusion with *wistly*, which was itself a corruption of the Middle-English *wisly*, certainly, verily, exactly. The sense which 'wistly' bears in two passages of Shakespeare (in whom alone and in the *Passionate Pilgrim* the word has been found) is 'attentively,' 'with scrutiny,' and this sense Skeat thinks may have arisen out of that of *wisly*. But in *Richard II*. v. 4. 7:

...speaking it, he wistly [Q. 2, wishtly] looked on me

As who should say 'I would thou wert the man' &c.;
and in *Passionate Pilgrim* VI. 12 the sense is more probably *wishfully, longingly*.

105.   **There.   Oft** Fraser MS.

nodding.   hoary, Fraser MS., with **spreading** and **nodding** super-scribed.

Gray wrote from Stoke to Walpole, Sept. 1737, a description of the now much frequented Burnham Beeches:

'I have at the distance of half-a-mile, through a green lane, a forest (the vulgar call it a common) all my own, at least as good as so, for I spy no human thing in it but myself. It is a little chaos of mountains and precipices; mountains, it is true, that do not ascend much above the clouds, nor are the declivities quite so amazing as Dover cliff; but just such hills as people who love their necks as well as I do may venture to climb, and craggs that give the eye as much pleasure as if they were dangerous: Both vale and hill are covered with most venerable beeches, and other very reverend vegetables, that, like most other ancient people, are always dreaming out their old stories to the winds:

> And as they bow their hoary tops relate,
> In murmuring sounds, the dark decrees of fate;
> While visions, as poetic eyes avow,
> Cling to each leaf, and swarm on every bough.

At the foot of one of these squats me I (il penseroso) and there grow to a trunk the whole morning.'

It was amid the same scenes that he wrote in 1742, *Ode on Spring* (13–15):

> "Where'er the rude and moss-grown beech
> O'ercanopies the glade
> Beside some water's rushy brink" &c.

which anticipate this place in the *Elegy*.

If the four verses in the letter to Walpole are not Gray's, I am unable to trace them. The first line illustrates the '*nodding* beech' of the *Elegy*. Cf. the Var. Lect. of Fraser MS. here.

106. Nowhere do beeches assume more 'fantastic' forms than at Burnham.

Luke compares Spenser, *Ruines of Rome*, stanza XXVIII, which combines Gray's scattered details, in the picture of an aged tree,

> "Lifting to heaven her aged *hoarie* head,
> Whose foot in ground hath left but feeble holde,
> But halfe disbowel'd lies above the ground,
> Showing her *wreathed* rootes" &c.

107, 108. "He lay along
> Under an oak, whose *antique root peep'd out*
> Upon the *brook* that brawls along this wood."
>
> *As You Like It* II. I. 30-32.

This is said of the melancholy Jaques, between whom and himself the melancholy and self-conscious Gray could scarcely fail, in a similar

scene, to make a fugitive comparison.   But, as he himself suggests to
Walpole, his nearer *analogue* in character is Milton's *Il Penseroso*:

'in close covert by some brook' &c.

babbles. Cf. (after Mitford) the 'loquaces lymphae' of Horace,
Carm. III. 13, 15.

109. **With gestures quaint now smileing** &c. Fraser MS.

'Smiling as in scorn' is certainly much like Jaques.

                 wayward fancies   ~~loved~~ would he
110. **Mutt'ring his fond conceits he ~~went to~~ rove:**

                                        Fraser MS.

would he, Egerton and Pembroke MSS.

       drooping,
111. **Now woeful wan, ~~he droop'd~~, as one forlorn.**

                                         Fraser MS.

I have printed 'woeful-wan' (with a hyphen) on the faith of
Mr Gosse, who professes to print from the edition of 1768. But
Dr Bradshaw affirms that there is no hyphen in the printed copies
published in Gray's lifetime. *Non nostrum inter vos* &c. The hyphen
is a mere convention, and it is admitted that it is found in the Pembroke
MS. here. Dr Bradshaw says "woful-wan means sad and pale, not
'wofully pale'." The second interpretation being just that which
the hyphen precludes, the hyphen is better retained.

113. **I. we** Fraser MS.

     Along the
114. **By the Heath-~~side~~ and at his fav'rite Tree.**

                                         Fraser MS.

116. **at.** **by** is written over this word in Fraser MS.

After 116 Gray began to write in Fraser MS.:

              There scattered oft the earliest,

but struck it through.

117. **due.** **meet,** Fraser MS.

118. **thro** has **by** written over it in Fraser MS.

the church-way path] Wakefield compares

          "the graves all gaping wide
          Every one lets forth his sprite
          In *the church-way paths* to glide."

            Shakespeare, *Mids. Night's Dream*, v. 1. 389.

Shakespeare's paths may be *in* the church-yard; the church-way paths
at Stoke Pogis are, as is common in country churches, paths from the
high-road to the churchyard, as Bradshaw notes.

119. **Approach and read, for thou canst read the Lay** Fraser

MS.; Gray's first meaning probably was only 'the Lay is there for any one to read.' But by bracketing 'for thou canst read' he has given the words more significance. As Professor Hales says "reading was not such a common accomplishment that it could be taken for granted." The 'hoary headed swain' is perhaps himself 'no scholar' (as he would put it), but presumes that the enquirer is more accomplished.

The change has the further advantage that Gray thus adopts a poetic device, such as Pope's

> "Tell (for you can) what is it to be wise."

> Pope, *Essay on Man*, IV. 260.

Or Young (quoted by Mitford without ref.):

> "And steal (for you can steal) celestial fire."

120. **Grav'd. Wrote** Fraser MS. with **Graved** and **carved** written over it.

that Fraser MS. with **yon** written over it.

121–124. That Gray was inclined to retain this stanza is probable because he has written over it in Pembroke MS. 'Insert.' And the stanza itself as it there appears is obviously written much later than the rest of the MS. for the ink is much darker. Gray has noted also "Omitted 1753." Dr Bradshaw has ascertained that it was first printed in the *third* edition of the *Elegy*, March 1751. Mason says it was omitted because Gray thought that it was "too long a parenthesis in this place." Dr Bradshaw adds "he may have noted the resemblance it bears to some expressions and lines in Collins' *Dirge in Cymbeline*, published 1747[1]":

> "To fair Fidele's grassy tomb
> 　　Soft maids and village hinds shall bring
> 　Each opening sweet of earliest bloom,
> 　　And rifle all the breathing spring.
>
> ·····································
>
> 　The redbreast oft, at evening hours,
> 　　Shall kindly lend his little aid,
> 　With hoary moss, and gathered flowers
> 　　To deck the ground where thou art laid."

That Gray had read these stanzas on their first appearance is perfectly certain, and the resemblance between the two pictures can scarcely be accidental. But, as usual, he condenses; and in describing his own grave, he has a modest regard for probability. The

---

[1] Really 1746, but dated 1747.

redbreast of Collins is the sympathetic bird of those "Babes in the Wood," who received no burial

> "Till Robin-red-breast piously
> Did cover them with leaves,"

which "little poetical ornament," says Addison in the *Spectator* (no. 85), "shews the genius of the author amidst all his simplicity, being just the same kind of fiction which Horace has made use of upon a parallel occasion in that passage where he describes himself, when he was a child, fallen asleep in a desert wood, and covered with leaves by the doves that took pity on him" (*Od.* III. 4. 959).

121. **Spring**, Fraser MS. with **Year** written above.

122. **frequent**, Fraser MS. with **Showers of** superscribed. **Vi'lets**, Fraser MS.

123. **Robin**, Fraser MS. **Redbreast** superscribed.

125. The Epitaph, which is not so headed in Fraser MS., is there written along the side of the page.

Ib.
> "how glad would lay me down
> As in my mother's lap."
>
> *Par. Lost* x. 777.
>
> Mitford.

126.
> 'he lived unknown
> To fame or fortune.'   *Agrippina*, ll. 39, 40.

127, 8. **Science**. See note on *Eton Ode* l. 3.

To these two lines it has been objected that they are obscurely expressed, and seem to combine a blessing and a curse as if they were cognate ideas. But Gray defines his melancholy to West, May 27, 1742 'Mine, you are to know, is a white Melancholy, or rather Leucocholy for the most part, which though it seldom laughs or dances, nor ever amounts to what one calls Joy or Pleasure, yet is a good easy sort of state' &c. His melancholy was closely connected with his studious retirement, and its nature is exactly fixed in these two lines. Milton's *Il Penseroso* is Gray all over, and it is noteworthy that whereas Milton is certainly indebted to the verses prefixed to Burton's *Anatomy of Melancholy* for his two companion poems, Burton has given to *his* melancholy man some of the pleasures which Milton has transferred to *L'Allegro*. Gray might say with La Fontaine:

> J'aime...les livres, la musique
> La ville et la campagne, enfin tout; il n'est rien,
> Qui ne me soit souverain bien,
> *Jusqu'aux sombres plaisirs d'un cœur mélancolique.*

127. frown'd not] Wakefield compares Horace IV. 3. 1, 2:

> " Quem tu Melpomene semel
> *Nascentem placido lumine videris* " &c.
> [He on whose birth the lyric Queen
> Of numbers smiled &c. Atterbury.]

129 sq. Very possibly, as Mitford seems to think, suggested by Cowley's lines on the death of Mr William Hervey (*Golden Treasury* CXXXVII.):

> " Large was his soul; as large a soul as e'er
> Submitted to inform a body here,
> High as the place 'twas shortly in Heaven to have
>   But low and humble as his grave;
> So high that all the virtues there did come.
>
> ....
>
> So low that for me too it made a room."

It is the same man, as described by himself and by 'the friend.'

soul. Heart, Fraser MS.

131, 132. "Much as I admire Gray, one feels I think, in reading his poetry never quite secure against the false poetical style of the eighteenth century. It is always near at hand, sometimes it breaks in; and the sense of this prevents the security one enjoys with truly classic work...

> 'Thy joys no glittering female meets—'
>
> [*Ode on Spring* l. 45.]

or even things in the *Elegy*:

> 'He gave to misery all he had—a tear;
>
> He gain'd from Heaven ('twas all he wish'd) a friend—'

are instances of the sort of drawback I mean." Matthew Arnold.

What Arnold notes is the affected antithesis and consequent exaggeration in 'all he had' and ''twas all he wished.' Add the straining after *point*. If his bounty was large, how comes it, the average reader asks, that he has only a tear to give to misery? If Heaven gave a large recompense, how came it that it gave him only one friend? The answer is that 'a tear ' *is* ' large bounty,' and that 'a friend' *is* 'a large recompense.' And the retort is that, if this is the point, it is badly made and is not worth making.

We ought not, perhaps, to seek too close a correspondence between the poet's circumstances and the epitaph. It is a coincidence which we must not press, that he was temporarily inconvenienced during the time when he was fitfully engaged upon the second half of the *Elegy* by the loss of a house (insured) in Cornhill; at no time in his life was he really embarrassed. During the same period also he had more than one true friend besides Wharton. One cannot however help suspecting either that this epitaph was the one part of the *Elegy* written in 1742, although undoubtedly not entered in the oldest extant MS. until the completion of the Poem, or that it is retrospective, and recalls the regrets of that melancholy year, when West was dead and Gray, then really solitary, may have longed to be with him (see *Odes* II. and III. Introductory notes). Both here and in the *Progress of Poesy* the 'personal note' with which a very general theme is made to end is distinctly *not* effective. Whether consciously or not, Gray in this imitates West, whose 'Muse as yet unheeded and unknown' winds up 'the monody on the Death of Queen Caroline' with a self-reference, the feebleness of which Gray would have recognised in the case of any other friend[1].

131. **all he had, a tear**] Gray here translates himself; the tribute to West's memory

> has lacrymas, memori quas ictus amore
> Fundo, *quod possum* &c.

(*'tis all I can*) in *De Principiis Cogitandi*, Lib. ii. 27, 28, written as he himself records in Pembroke MS., at Stoke, June, 1742; this tends to confirm the notion that to this date belongs at any rate the *inspiration* of the Epitaph. It is a tribute to the Lucretianism of Gray's Latin lines that Mitford here attributes them to Lucretius.

> think
> 134, 135. **Nor seek to draw them from their dread abode**
> (**His Frailties there in trembling Hope repose**)
>
> Fraser MS.
>
> 135.   —paventosa speme.
>
> Petrarch, *Son.* 114, Gray.

The Sonnet is No. 97 in ed. Giacomo Leopardi, Florence 1847, l. 12 'freddo foco e *paventosa speme*,' said by Petrarch of his love kept in check by Laura. Gray might have found the same expression nearer home in a more apposite context, e.g. Hooker, *Ecclesiastical Polity* B. I. xi. [6] where it is said that Hope's highest object is 'that everlasting Goodness which in Christ doth quicken the dead,' and that she 'begins here with a *trembling expectation* of things far removed and as yet but only heard of' &c.

There is, however, surely a boldness the reverse of happy as well as some confusion of thought in speaking of a man's frailties as reposing in

---

[1] See *Gray and His Friends*, pp. 14, 114.

trembling hope on the bosom of God. The words of Gray himself to Mason recur to the mind 'all I can say is that your elegy should not end with the worst line in it.'

Printed in the United States
By Bookmasters